Thomas Maude studied at the European Centre for Craftsmen in Venice and has held the William Morris Craft Fellowship. He has worked as a stone-mason on some of Europe's most prestigious restoration projects, including Salisbury Cathedral and Wells Cathedral.

'An excellent new book . . . Written by master mason Thomas Maude, it tells you how to zip straight into the world of the masons and carpenters who constructed the building. Most guidebooks are as dry as the bones under the cathedral floor. Not Maude's book. As a master mason, he knows that stones can speak. Better still, he wants us to know what they are saying . . . His method is simple: follow his guide and you will know the building inside out by the time you leave.' Giles Milton, *Mail on Sunday*

'His inside information means he can cast a new light on some very familiar places.' *Independent on Sunday*

'A good companion for those who want to understand more about Britain's cathedrals, abbeys and churches.' *Financial Times*

Tauris Parke Paperbacks is an imprint of I.B.Tauris. It is dedicated to publishing books in accessible paperback editions for the serious general reader within a wide range of categories, including biography, history, travel and the ancient world. The list includes select, critically acclaimed works of top quality writing by distinguished authors that continue to challenge, to inform and to inspire. These are books that possess those subtle but intrinsic elements that mark them out as something exceptional.

The Colophon of Tauris Parke Paperbacks is a representation of the ancient Egyptian ibis, sacred to the god Thoth, who was himself often depicted in the form of this most elegant of birds. Thoth was credited in antiquity as the scribe of the ancient Egyptian gods and as the inventor of writing and was associated with many aspects of wisdom and learning.

GUIDED BY A STONE-MASON

Exploring the Cathedrals, Abbeys and Churches of Britain

Thomas Maude

TPP

TAURIS PARKE
PAPERBACKS

New edition published in 2010 by Tauris Parke Paperbacks
An imprint of I.B.Tauris and Co Ltd
6 Salem Road, London W2 4BU
175 Fifth Avenue, New York NY 10010
www.ibtauris.com

Distributed in the United States and Canada Exclusively by Palgrave Macmillan
175 Fifth Avenue, New York NY 10010

First published in 1997 by I.B.Tauris & Co Ltd

Copyright © 1997, 2010 Thomas Maude

Cover image: Wells Cathedral © Pitkin Guides Ltd

ISBN: 978 1 84885 547 2

A full CIP record for this book is available from the British Library
A full CIP record is available from the Library of Congress

Library of Congress Catalog Card Number: available

Printed and bound in India by Replika Press Pvt. Ltd.

Contents

GUIDED BY A STONE-MASON

8

Preface

A FORCE-TEN GALE is blowing, the temperature is minus 8, and I am on top of a swaying scaffold, suspended 108 feet above the ground. The weather is cruel and unforgiving. It is mid-February and the top of the south-west tower of Wells Cathedral is not a place for the faint-hearted. I remember the many times when people have said to me, 'Your job must be really enjoyable and satisfying'. Their words ring in ears as chilled as the north-east wind that whistles through them. Clothed in every ounce of wool I can find, and tied to the scaffold by a rope around my waist as a crude safety measure, it's time to start work.

The thought that my forebears were up here actually building this tower nearly eight centuries ago is never far from my mind. To be so close to their work evokes a powerful feeling of their presence, and for a moment the unfriendly elements seem to melt away and warmth is breathed into my eyes and hands in anticipation of the labours ahead. Old decayed stone has been removed and new stone fixed into position. It now waits to be carved to match the original shape and form.

I am armed with tools that a medieval mason would immediately recognise and which he could easily pick up and use: a large cone-shaped mallet made of apple wood; a range of chisels with names like boaster, pitcher, claw, mitre, quirker, punch; and of course the set-square and dividers which are still seen as the emblem of the freemasons, confirmation of their deep-rooted origins in the craft of masonry.

The only difference between me freezing on this building today and my medieval counterpart is that he would either have been pulling parsnips in the fields or sitting safely in a mason's lodge carving stones for use later in the year, for in those times no major work on buildings was carried out between November and April and, with the exception of the most highly-skilled craftsmen, all labour was laid off for the winter.

But sunnier memories are never far away from me, for like the journeymen craftsmen throughout the centuries, I had once taken to the road with my tools on my back. Like them, I had headed for the Continent and into the unknown; in search of work, knowledge, experience and, of course, adventure. For a time the sky-scapes of Venice, Rome, Jerusalem, Egypt and many other places became familiar to me as I helped restore the wonderful stone structures that lay within them. My journey began in the north of Italy among the churches and palaces of the most serene city of all, Venice. Here I studied at the European Centre for Craftsmen and learned from fifty of the finest craftsmen (and craftswomen) brought together from every corner of Europe – masons, wood-carvers, fresco painters, blacksmiths, goldsmiths, stuccoists and sculptors. Each expert brought his or her own special skill and experience, language and culture, all blending together to form a truly intoxicating mixture.

Here at the crossroads of Europe I began to realise how the medieval craft guilds had been formed and why they were so important for the transference of skills from generation to generation. After my previous six years' apprenticeship in England, I had been left with a thousand unanswered questions about the buildings on which I had worked. Now the language of architecture was magically transformed from the complex terminolology used by historians and academics into a tangible clarity that suddenly burst into life for me. It became a language spoken by craftsmen for craftsmen and, irrespective of which nation a person was from, it could be understood by all. Slowly but surely the many pieces of the architectural jigsaw were put into place.

Finally it was time to move on. With tools once again slung across my back I travelled further into Europe and on to the Middle East, working anywhere that serendipity took me – from the Presidential Palace in Rome to a mosque in Jerusalem and the temples of Luxor in Egypt. Each city, each country, each culture and each experience added to the richness of learning and left its mark upon me as clear and incised as a freshly-carved stone. Eventually I turned for home, arriving with a box full of tools, a far greater understanding of the buildings of England, and a profound sense of admiration for the journeymen masons of the past.

Once again it is time to start on a journey. This time it's a journey of exploration about the medieval cathedrals, abbeys and churches of Britain. But on this occasion we are going to make it together. The restoration of these wonderful and awe-inspiring buildings has been my work for the last twenty years and it is my privilege, as a stone-mason, to share with you the secrets that lie within them.

Wells Cathedral: corbel

Have you ever listened to Luciano Pavarotti singing opera in his native Italian and thought how wonderful it sounded, although you didn't understand a word? The style and form of a building can often seem the same: you love the building but haven't a clue as to what it's all about. If you follow me, I guarantee that the short steps we take together will soon become giant strides in your understanding of medieval buildings; we may not reach Pavarotti's fluency and clarity, but we can at least share in the marvel that is the discovery of history.

GUIDED BY A STONE-MASON

Introduction

A THOUSAND YEARS AGO at the close of the first millennium most people throughout Western Europe believed that the world would come to an end. As this date came and went and no such catastrophe occurred there was the most amazing new beginning.

The Dark Ages covered the time period between approximately 450 (the fall of the Western Roman Empire) and 1000. Not all historians like the term 'Dark Ages' to describe this span of years. Half say that it means Europe was a backward, barbarous place for nearly all that time: the other half say this was not so and there were great achievements made during this period.

I have lived and worked in Rome and seen at first hand how Ancient Rome was built – stone upon stone – and followed its building techniques. A monumental civilisation was created which had dynamism, invention, and the will to expand and develop its culture. When the Roman Empire fell all this collapsed. It was this lack of advancement – a combination of the end of development and evolution of tried and tested ideas and the lack of confidence to push through a progressive plan – that was the most significant theme of the Dark Ages.

The Roman Empire had been like a huge fountain-head with a high pressure of water forced through it, and when it fell so did the pressure; not completely, but to a mere trickle compared with what had gone before. In fact, apart from the vision of the Emperor Charlemagne (742-814) there is precious little else that we can actually call a confident forward-looking culture in Europe. There were a

Opposite: *Castle Acre Priory, Norfolk*

Exeter Cathedral: 'a flowering of the human spirit'

few isolated pockets of enlightenment in such places as Lindisfarne and Iona in Scotland, and in Ireland too, where the beautiful *Book of Kells* was produced, but such places were few and far between.

So what relevance does this have for the medieval church buildings we can see and enjoy today? Well, it gives us a vital insight into 'Why?' and 'How?' A new impetus was born after the year 1000 that allowed these mighty stone giants to rise. If we imagine Europe as a fertile piece of land, then under the Ancient Romans it had produced a high-yield bumper harvest. After the collapse of the Western Roman Empire the land lay fallow and inert for five centuries. Then came a new boom, possibly the greatest surge of confidence ever known. Of all the great abbeys, cathedrals and churches that we can see today, not one of them had a stone laid above ground level before our starting date of the year 1000.

Only a hundred years on, throughout Europe and especially in Britain, following the Norman Conquest in 1066, there had been an extraordinary change in every branch of life – action, philosophy, organisation and technology. There was a thaw from the cold years of the Dark Ages, and a new flowering of the human spirit. This immense surge of activity is visible to us today in the abbey and cathedral buildings that flourished as a result. By the year 1100 many of the major cathedrals such as Durham, Ely, Norwich, Westminster, Southwell, Gloucester, Rochester, Hereford, Worcester, Canterbury, Winchester and Exeter had their foundations laid and the buildings were rising steadily in the Norman-French style.

Why had such a monumental change taken place almost within a single lifetime? There are many possible answers to that question, but one stands out as more important than any other. The triumph of the Church.

The Church was basically a law unto itself, growing and attracting wealth, conserving and expanding its properties. Men of intelligence were taking holy orders and rising from obscurity to positions of immense influence. In short the Church, directed from Rome, had become the overpowering dominating influence throughout Britain and Europe, and its power and wealth were now to be turned into a visible expression of its dominance. And so out of the cluster of ramshackle timber houses began to rise the mighty stone monuments we can still see today.

CHAPTER ONE

The Norman Cathedral

W HETHER VISITING a majestic cathedral, a vast abbey or a small parish church, we need something to start us on our way of unravelling and understanding what these buildings are all about. This starting point is the arch. The arch will become our key to clarity. Initially only one question needs to be asked. *Is the arch rounded or pointed?*

THE ROUND ARCH

T HE ROUND ARCH was invented and perfected by the Romans and was brought to Britain by their conquering legions. After the departure of the Romans, the round arch continued to be used

Hales Church, Norfolk, a Norman or Romanesque arch
Previous page: Norwich Cathedral

THE NORMAN CATHEDRAL

here by successive invaders – the Angles and Saxons – until just after the Norman Conquest. Only rarely do examples remain of this early Roman and Saxon architecture.

For the most dramatic use and development of the round arch we will start by looking at some of the cathedrals and abbeys built in Britain in the thirty-four years between the Norman Conquest in 1066 and the very important year of 1100. The Normans brought not only their language, laws and culture, but also their way of building known either as 'Norman' or 'Romanesque' since this Norman style was itself based on the Roman one. It was characterised by round arches, massive circular pillars and thick walls. Among the best examples in England are the cathedrals at Winchester, Ely, Gloucester and Durham. In fact almost all Britain's major cathedrals contain some degree of the Norman style left for us to see today.

PLAN OF A CATHEDRAL

BEFORE WE ENTER one of these mighty structures, let's first learn how to orientate ourselves. From the grandest cathedrals to the most humble of parish churches, they almost all follow the same basic plan of a Latin Cross. With few exceptions, the altar and nave are aligned along an east-to-west axis. The origin of this plan is very

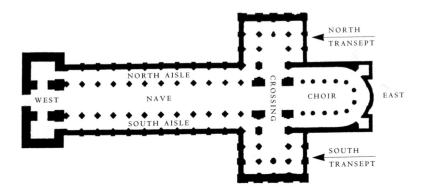

PLAN OF A CATHEDRAL

obvious when it is realised that the Latin Cross represents Christ's Crucifixion. The doorway through which we enter at the west end of the long nave represents Christ's pierced feet; His legs are the nave; the transepts are His open arms; while the altar at the east end represents Christ's head, physically pointing eastwards to Jerusalem, the site of the Crucifixion.

CATHEDRALS, like the abbey churches of monasteries, were not designed as buildings where ordinary people could go and worship. That was the role of parish churches. Instead a cathedral was built to the glory of God and was the seat of the bishop, where the ordained offered prayers and worship almost continually around the clock. The people were allowed into the nave during services, but only on sufferance. Indeed the nave, although frequently the largest part of the church, was not even considered sacred ground until the last century or so. In medieval times the screen between the eastern end and the nave provided a physical as well as spiritual barrier separating the clergy from the laity.

SUPPOSE THAT we are standing outside the west front of a church and are about to enter through the west door to get to the beginning of the nave. As an example I am going to take you into Durham Cathedral, but it could equally well be any cathedral or even your own parish church. We are now standing at the entrance to the nave, looking down the whole interior to the eastern end and the altar. It's at this point that we can easily become overwhelmed by the sheer size, height and complexity of what is laid out before us. If you are, then take heart, because one of the original aims of this and indeed any cathedral was to impose just such a feeling on anyone who entered. Imagine a group of medieval peasants standing in our place. They live in squalid timber huts; overcrowded, dark, wretched and poor. They gaze in amazement at what towers over and in front of them, and are left in no doubt as to the majesty of God, and the

Durham: the nave arcade, early 12th century

power, wealth and dominance that is 'the Church'. Nine centuries have passed since then, but that same message still holds, fascinates and humbles us today.

I suggest that we first sit for a while, in one of the seats only a few steps from where we are standing, and gradually take in all that is around us. The first things we notice at eye level are the long rows of massive round pillars to the left (north) and right (south) of us, rolling down the length of the nave and rising to support the round arches that sit upon them. The whole of this row of pillars and arches is called the 'nave arcade'.

THE PIER (PILLAR)

THESE IMMENSE drum-shaped pillars at Durham, also called piers, are nearly seven feet in diameter and are typical of the Norman style. The Normans always built stoutly and simply, with an eye to solid construction as their first priority, which today leaves us with a feeling of heaviness. The surface stones of these piers have been shaped with an axe from square blocks of sandstone so that each face is curved to fit the circle. The backs of the stone would be left rough to create a good bonding surface. The central core of each pier is made of crushed waste stone and the whole is held together with good lime mortar. The cut stones with the infill have been placed on top of each other to reach the required height. The shape of the piers which are a true circle and the arches above them which are a true semi-circle give us the unique and unmistakable geometry of Norman building.

If the weight and breadth of these piers leave us in any doubt that they are Norman, then we have two further clues close at hand: the capital – the stone that sits directly above and on top of the pier; and the designs and decorations that are cut into the masonry of the pier itself.

Durham: each axe-carved pier is alternated with a cluster or compound pier

THE CAPITAL

Generally, the first thing we notice when we look at a capital is the decoration carved on its surface; here at Durham, however, the decoration on the piers is so striking that the capitals are deliberately left plain. The major function of the capital is to act as a cushion between the pier below, and the arch-springing masonry above. This function determines the distinctive wider top and narrower bottom that shapes the basic form of the capital. Early

Norman capitals. Opposite: *Durham*
Clockwise from top left: *Compton Martin, Somerset; Sutton Bingham, Dorset; Gloucester Cathedral; Kilpeck, Herefordshire*

Norman carving is described by academics as 'rude' (a word meaning simple, unskilful, or unimaginative). Having carved a variety of these capitals myself, I would like to refer to them merely as 'simple' – by contrast with complex ornate designs found elsewhere – since they certainly require skill.

NORMAN DECORATION

THESE ARE SOME of the major motifs that you will find enriching the doorways, piers, round arches and capitals of Norman design around the country. They were used not only in the great

Hales Church, Norfolk: the zigzag patterns or chevrons are the most distinctive of Norman decorations

cathedrals and abbeys, but also in parish and village churches built around the year 1100. In fact, it is in the smaller local churches that their use lingered on for at least another century.

The method used by the stone-masons for carving these early Norman details was known as 'axe-work'. A series of large and small axes were used to shape the stone. It seems that the mallet and chisel were used only for the intricate carvings set above a doorway or for the capitals in later Norman work. The stone for a capital would first be shaped by axe to measure for its place in the building. Then when the stone was fixed in position it was carved with the mallet and chisel to a highly ornamental finish.

Malmesbury Abbey, Wiltshire

BLIND ARCADING

THIS IS ANOTHER distinctive feature of the Norman style. It is the decorative use of the column and round arch, serving no structural function. We will find it both inside and outside the building, built against a plain stone wall. Its effect when simply used is striking, and when used with heavy ornament it can be quite dramatic.

COLOUR IN CATHEDRALS – AND CHURCHES

B RIGHT VIVID COLOURS were painted on to the stonework of all medieval cathedrals (both Norman and Gothic). Reds, blues, greens and yellow ochre were all obtained by mixing earth pigments, and where finances permitted gold leaf was also used. The dark Norman interiors relied on these colours to brighten the gloom and provide a striking impact. Simple but effective decoration and designs were painted on the capitals, piers, arches and other features, such as the blind arcading that ran along the side aisle walls. Where there was a large expanse of flat wall a more substantial composition could be painted and here there would have been pictures of Christ, Our Lady and the saints.

The technique of painting walls is known as 'fresco' and it was perfected and brought to Britain by the Romans. 'True fresco' means covering the stone walls with a coat of lime plaster that must be painted on the same day it is applied so that the paint soaks into the wet plaster for approximately one or two inches. When the plaster dries the colour is 'fixed' permanently. Unfortunately in Britain this technique was seldom used and instead the lime plaster was allowed to dry first and was then painted, so the colours were only superficially applied to the surface. The result was that with time these wall paintings peeled off and few have survived for us to see today.

Polychrome (many coloured) decoration was not just confined to the interior. Most exterior façades, especially the important west fronts where visitors were received, were painted. (At Wells and Lincoln cathedrals many traces of the original colours were found during recent restoration.) The effect of seeing these colossal buildings in the sunlight, and alone in their grandeur, must have been truly astonishing for the medieval pilgrims.

UPPER STOREYS: THE TRIFORIUM

I F WE NOW LOOK HIGHER, we can see another row of smaller and
more slender piers, again with a row of round arches that roll
down the length of the nave. This has the delightful name of the
triforium gallery. The origin of this name is not clear, but there are at

*Durham: the nave arcade with the triforium above and
light shining through the clerestory*

least two possible explanations. One, that it derives from the French *trés-forces* which relates to the three (*trés*) openings into which each bay is divided (a bay being the space between each major pier). This theory cannot be right because most Norman triforium bays are divided into two or four. The second and most likely is that it could be a corruption or rather misreading of *Tribunum* which used to be the name given to an elevated chamber inside a church.

Sometimes the gallery of the triforium is quite large and light as at Gloucester Cathedral, while at Lincoln it is of sufficiently great size that it contained an altar where a priest and congregation could celebrate Mass.

The main reason for this gallery was initially structural. If we could stand in the passageway behind the triforium arches, we would not be above the central nave, but over one of the side aisles, and above our heads would be the sloping timber roof of the side aisle. This passageway therefore allowed workmen access to repair this sloping roof, or the upper walls of the nave. Apart from the arches through to the body of the church, and a door at each end for access, there were no other openings or windows in the triforium: it is there-fore a dark passageway.

A good guide to remember is that a church or cathedral will only have a triforium gallery if it has vaulted side aisles, and this is why small parish churches rarely have this intermediate stage.

UPPER STOREYS: THE CLERESTORY

STILL SITTING at the west end of the nave, if we look even higher up the walls we see a third row of piers and arches, the 'clerestory'. The first thing we notice here is how light it is, natural light that is, which also illuminates the name. It is the 'clear storey', one of the few places where natural light entered.

The Norman cathedral was rather a gloomy, poorly-lit place. In the major churches there would be thick, opaque, stained glass, but in parish churches the windows would rarely be glazed – because of the expense and rarity of glass – and although they might have wooden shutters, they were usually open to the elements.

Never be in a hurry to move on from your seat. Instead, we are going to pause for a moment and take in the full splendour of the nave. If we could reach out and touch the details we have been looking at then our natural instinct would be to handle them, feeling for shapes and textures that are the great attraction of natural stone and the fascinating carved patterns that bring it to life. The longer we linger and use our eyes in this way, then the more the building will speak to us.

THE NAVE ROOF – VAULTING IN STONE

WHEN WE HAVE examined the three levels of the nave walls here at Durham Cathedral – the arcading, the triforium and the clerestory – our eyes naturally look up to the roof and the amazing sight of vaulting in stone. The setting-out and execution of early medieval stone vaulting is complex but gives us a fascinating insight into how churches, both large and small, changed from the heavy dim interiors of the Norman style into the tall light and more airy, later Gothic structures. We are now going to cut through this complexity and step by simple step reveal one of the greatest technological innovations of this or any age.

UP UNTIL THE YEAR 1100 the medieval builder had only ever used the round arch, passed on to him from the Ancient Romans. The reason Norman buildings have such solidity and massiveness was the limitation that a round arch imposed. To vault in stone over a space as high and wide as a nave roof was very difficult. The Romans did build vaults over small areas using a semi-circular 'tunnel' vault, which as its name suggests was tunnel shaped and straight. When two tunnel vaults met at the crossing this produced a groined vault, the groin being the sharp edge. At least two thousand years ago the Romans first used the technique of groined vaulting and they refined it to a high degree. But the skill and knowledge to advance it even further did not arrive in Europe for another eight hundred years. This momentous achievement was the forming of the first pointed arch, brought about by the daring and adventurous use of the most important advance in building technology – ribbed vaulting.

THE FIRST RIBBED VAULTING AND POINTED ARCH

I HAVE MENTIONED that a dramatic change occurred in the design of churches about the year 1100. It is therefore no accident that I have brought you to look at the vaulted interior of Durham Cathedral, for it was here that the first ribbed vault and pointed arch was formed.

Durham: the full impact of the nave, looking from west to east

Many claims to this invention have been made from all over Europe – especially from France – but as an English stone-mason it is only natural that I am proud to claim its birth here. Although we don't know the name of the master-mason at Durham who first used it, there is good evidence that he may have been of Norman-French origin. Pointed arches were used widely in Islamic building, such as the great mosque at Damascus, as early as the 6th century and so it would be more accurate to say they were introduced to Europe at Durham rather than invented.

So why was ribbed vaulting so special? Well, to find the answer you could go away and read many articles on this subject, running into dozens of volumes and a mountain of facts and figures. This will probably leave you completely dazed by the variety and complexity of this 12th century state-of-the-art technology. I suggest you come with me and learn the basic terms, coupled with a general rule-of-thumb layout which you can then apply to the hundreds of variations that occur in ribbed vaulting around the country – and of course, through-out Europe.

The great disadvantage of a groined vault was that it was not self-supporting. In other words, if you take away the stone work from between the groins, then the vault would fall down. A ribbed vault is just the opposite: *it is self-supporting*. That means that if we take away all the stone work that lies between the ribs, the vault would still stand up on its own. This last fact is the fundamental principle of both vaulting and the whole basis of the Gothic architecture of the centuries since. Namely that only the ribs are of importance in holding the structure up, compared with the Norman style of architecture where the thickness and bulk of the walls and surrounding masonry were all necessary for this purpose.

This self-supporting rib vault opened up all kinds of exciting possibilities, the most important of which was the ability to increase by a small amount the angle at which each rib was sprung (originated at the lower end). The result was that where the ribs met at the top the vault became pointed. This modification of the vaulting was first used at the east end of Durham Cathedral in 1098, and by about 1130 it had been extended to the vaulting of the whole of the nave.

THE START OF THE GOTHIC STYLE

THE INTRODUCTION of the pointed arch marked the end of the heavy Romanesque style of building and started – tentatively at first – the lighter, taller and most common form of church building that we see today, the Gothic style. The old style didn't end abruptly, but lingered on in minor churches for another hundred years or so, as did its decoration. But as the ribbed vault made its presence felt throughout the country, it soon swept all before it. How many master-masons made the long journey to Durham to see this new style for themselves, and being satisfied with what they saw, were happy to return and use it in their latest building? Naves of new churches that had been conceived in a Romanesque style to take a timber roof were soon changed, and a pointed stone vault was thrown across its open space instead.

We are going to look now at how these vaults were made: naming the details, noting how they fitted together, and how they flowered into the Gothic style. From where we are sitting at the west end of Durham Cathedral it is possible to see them all. It is a bit like look-ing up at the sky on a clear night. Initially it looks very complex, but when the major stars and constellations are pointed out, then the whole panorama takes on an illuminated quality.

Each stone that makes up the four cross ribs in a vault is called a *voussoir*, a French word meaning wedge-shaped. Where the last voussoirs meet at the top of the vault we have one stone with four faces waiting to receive the thrust of the four ribs. This is called a 'boss' or a 'keystone'. When making a vault, the masons would first build the required shape in wood, a 'former', and place it in the desired position. Each voussoir would then be laid on the former until

Durham: one of the first ribbed vaults.
The rib that stretches from pier to pier is a transverse rib.
The four cross ribs rise to the central boss

THE NORMAN CATHEDRAL

they reached the top. The boss was then placed in position directly in the centre, marrying the four faces of each of the top voussoirs and so closing the vault. Then after three 'Hail Marys' and four 'Our Fathers' the wooden former would be taken away and the four ribs stayed up all on their own. The spaces between these ribs were filled with as light a stone as possible, and then covered with lime plaster.

This then is the most basic form of a vault. There are literally hundreds of variations, but they all follow the same basic plan of construction. Much later the master-mason was to demonstrate his skill and design flair by building vaults that were so complicated as to dazzle and overwhelm even the most knowledgeable of scholars at first glance. This is fan vaulting, and is something that we shall look at in more detail later. For now there are only two more important details we need to know.

At the point where the vault begins (or springs) — usually the triforium wall — there is a small capital stone on which the first voussoir sits, ready to start the procession of the other voussoirs upwards and towards the central boss. This first voussoir is known to masons as a 'springer'. Originally the springers of adjacent vaults vied for position on the same capital, and unless they were extremely accurately positioned it made a weak point in the structure. It was soon realised that the capital and the lowest voussoirs could be carved out of one stone, eliminating this weakness in design. In fact, several of these complex stones were employed one above the other — known as a *tas de charge* — before the voussoirs finally disengaged to radiate to their respective ribs.

Here at Durham you will notice that there is no *tas de charge* stone. This is because the design wasn't invented until after Durham was finished.

Now we have constructed a simple stone vault we are going to look at how the addition of detail can turn it into a complex web of breathtaking beauty.

The ridge ribs were the first to be introduced, and as their name

*Gloucester Cathedral: vaulted ceiling showing clearly transverse, cross
and ridge ribs with added tiercons and liernes*

suggests they ran along the ridge of the vault – the highest part –
connecting up all the boss stones. These were soon followed by a
new type of rib that started from the same *tas de charge* as the earlier
cross ribs, but instead of going to the bosses they went to some
point on the ridge ribs. Since these were the third type of rib to be
introduced (after the transverse and ridge ones), they are known as
tierceron ribs, from the French word *tierce* meaning third. These three
types of rib can all be considered essential to the structure of the

stone vault. The final type to be employed was purely decorative, and is known as a lierne rib. *Lier* is from the French word meaning to tie, and that is exactly what these ribs do, they 'tie' other ribs together. They can be placed anywhere in the vault, between or connecting with any of the other ribs.

The addition of the lierne ribs enabled masons to create a very complex form of interconnections that would eventually lead to the exquisitely beautiful conclusion of fan vaulting. King Henry VII's Chapel at Westminster Abbey is still vaulting in stone, but here we have reached the ultimate expression of the master-mason's art. Other good examples are at King's College, Cambridge and Sherborne Abbey, Dorset.

Once you have seen the spectacular beauty of this fan vaulting, you may feel a little overawed by its apparent complexity. But if you think of how the design of these vaults progressed, you can now recognise the original cross ribs springing from the *tas de charges* and going diagonally across each vault to meet in the middle at the boss. Next you can see the ridge ribs going along the top of each vault and joining up the bosses. Then there are the lierne ribs springing from the same *tas de charges* but going up to meet the ridge ribs. The rest of the ribs are the tiercerons or tying ribs. You understand now how the medieval masons achieved this wonderful effect.

To sum up our visit to Durham, Norman or Romanesque work should bring to mind heaviness, solidity, round arches, thick massive pillars, dim interiors, small windows, masons cutting stones with axes, and French-speaking master-masons and bishops. These are the things that pass through my mind whenever and wherever I see Norman work. It could be a whole nave in a cathedral, or it could be just one simple capital in my local church that has survived the centuries. The feeling is always the same: excitement, history, and a hidden language waiting to be read.

CHAPTER TWO

The Gothic Cathedral

W E NOW LEAVE BEHIND us the world of the Norman builder and advance to the Gothic style to try and discover why it became so dominant in church building for the next 500 years. We are going to move southwards to look at two cathedrals which have no Romanesque work in them at all – Wells and Salisbury. Both cathedrals were conceived and built in the new pointed arch Gothic style.

If we enter Wells Cathedral and, as at Durham, seat ourselves at the rear of the building, when we look down the length of the nave we cannot fail to notice how light and airy everything is. As our eyes turn to the walls on each side and look up at the piers, the triforium and the clerestory, we note that there is not a hint of a round arch to be seen anywhere. Everything is pointed, more slender, and lighter.

Now let's walk down the centre of the nave towards the east end. We notice that there are two smaller naves running parallel to our central one: on our left is the north aisle, and on our right is the south aisle. It is worth going to look at them in closer detail. The name aisle which derives from the Latin word *ala* meaning wing was chosen by the early builders to reflect the wings of a bird folded alongside the body of a bird at rest. These side aisles are almost invariably vaulted, and here at Wells the simplicity, gracefulness and light feeling of the ribbed vaults is quite simply breathtaking. Wells is relatively small and therefore has an intimacy to it compared with the rather intimidating feel of larger cathedrals. The aisles and nave seem tangible and close to the eye, and these vaults, set as they are against a white lime plaster background, pick out and emphasise their ribs and bosses with a refreshing clarity. The intricate, fine scrollwork around the bosses in the nave is painted on to the plaster.

The piers separating the aisles from the nave have also changed in shape and size from the earlier Norman style. They have developed to

Previous page: *Salisbury Cathedral from the west*

Photograph © Judyth Platt/Adams Picture Library

*Wells: symmetrical perfection of transverse and cross ribs
using the new* tas-de-charges *springers*

become much lighter, with small multishafts instead of one huge cylindrical drum.

We also notice that the shape of the capitals is different, and so is the decoration on them. There are beautifully carved forms of

Wells: pure Early English Gothic; the nave arcade

leaves, curving back upon themselves to create shadow and depth. This is exactly the effect that the mason had in mind when he carved them. The name for this type of carving is 'Early English Stiff Leaf'.

Wells: capital with Early English Stiff Leaf carving

The natural world that surrounded the medieval craftsman had an immense impact on him. The shape and forms of flora and fauna were his inspiration and being unable to read and write only accentuated this influence of Nature. Whatever material the craftsmen worked in, plants and animals gave them the ideas they needed to create forms and details of true beauty. This influence of Nature is frequently noticed by ordinary people, including children, and recognised for what it is, a simple message that has been communicated down the centuries.

Ahead of us as we continue eastwards is the vast space or 'crossroads' within a cathedral known as the crossing and transepts.

THE CROSSING AND TRANSEPTS

A TRANSEPT means anything that spans and crosses over, and that is exactly what it does here in the cathedral – crossing over our straight path along the nave to the altar at the east end. The north and south transepts, respectively to our left and right, are outstretched arms. Usually they are of equal length and size, at least in their original construction they were, but in many cathedrals and churches one or other was subsequently extended in length. In a small parish church the transepts may only be a few feet in length, but here in a cathedral such as Wells they are much larger and grander.

In any church this crossing is a very dynamic place, but in a cathedral it is especially so. We are now going to stand in the centre of the crossing. This means that we have the central tower both physically and geometrically directly above us. Here at Wells it is not as large as most, so we are going to transfer ourselves to that of its close neighbour Salisbury where we have not only a massive tower but one of the highest spires in Europe.

We are standing in this position at the centre of the crossing and looking upward for a particular reason. If you put yourself in the place of the master-mason responsible for building this cathedral, you can see some of the problems confronting him. (Ladies can take heart from the large number of fine women stone-masons that now work as master-masons in cathedrals today, producing some of the best work to come out of cathedral workshops around the country.)

The master-mason at Salisbury Cathedral was responsible for the structural stability of the four corner piers that hold up the tower and spire above. He also had to bear in mind that the collapse of towers and vaults in medieval times was a common and often fatal occurrence. If you look up at the shafts of the columns at Salisbury you will see they bend outwards by nearly two feet. If they bend any more, then the whole of the tallest spire in England may come crashing down. The mason either had to start dismantling all the stone

Salisbury: the discreet solution of the strainer arch between the two piers of the crossing, 15th century

THE CROSSING AND TRANSEPTS

work already built, or think up something else quickly to remedy the situation.

At Wells Cathedral in the year 1338 the master-mason suddenly saw that the tower had started to lean and crack and that the foundations were beginning to give way, all because the tower was built higher than originally intended.

In both present-day Wells and Salisbury Cathedrals you can see the emergency solutions which were arrived at by the respective masons. On three sides at Wells were inserted the dramatic 'Strainer Arch', a huge scissor-shape that strengthens the crossing piers and also distributes the extra load from the heightened tower. At Salisbury the emergency solution was more discreet, whilst still serving the same purpose. Both cathedrals clearly show us that each master-mason solved problems in his own unique way – and they worked.

THE EASTERN END OF THE CATHEDRAL

WITH THE NAVE and crossing behind us, we are now about to enter the most historic, holy and fascinating part of the cathedral. But before we do, let's look first at the history that surrounds the whole of this eastern end, and also the different parts contained within it; the choir, presbytery, sanctuary and ambulatory. All cathedrals were built so the eastern end was completed first. As soon as the sanctuary had been raised and roofed, it was immediately consecrated. It was then opened for pilgrims to visit without hardly a stone being laid in the nave; in fact a significant part of the cost of the latter would be funded from the offerings of the pilgrims.

The word 'cathedral' originates from the Greek *cathedra*, meaning a throne or seat. A cathedral is both literally and physically the 'seat' of the bishop, being both the mother-church at the centre of a bishop's

Opposite: *Wells – the crossing showing the radical solution of the scissor-shaped strainer arch used by the master-mason, c 1338-48*

diocese, as well as a building containing a large and ornate bishop's throne in the sanctuary area. All cathedrals were staffed and run by a group of clergy called a chapter, headed by a dean.

Cathedrals originated as either 'regular' or 'secular' and there is an important distinction between them.

If the cathedral was a regular one it was part of a monastery. The clergy were monks and lived by a monastic Rule (Latin *regulus*). They took little notice of what took place in the world outside the confines of their monastery and cathedral church, and were totally bound by their monastic rules and regulations. Regular cathedrals include Durham, Ely, Winchester, Canterbury, Peterborough, Bristol, Chester, Southwark, Worcester, Carlisle, Norwich, Rochester, Gloucester and St Albans.

If a cathedral was secular (from the Latin word meaning living out in the world) then the clergy would live, work, and administer the cathedral from specially-erected (non-monastic) buildings adjacent to the church. We still see these today in the form of a cathedral close or precinct, as at York, Wells, Chichester, Salisbury, Exeter, Hereford and Lincoln.

As many of our cathedrals were monastic or regular in origin, this had a direct effect on how the whole eastern end of the church developed from its simple origins into the elaborate structure we see before us today. These origins take us back to the very first Christian churches founded in Rome around the year 400, which used the same shape, and indeed the same name, as the pagan Roman 'basilica'. In Ancient Rome the basilica was large, and internally there would be two rows of columns stretching the length of the main aisle. Its original use was for business, for exchange and for law; the semi-circular apse being the area where the seat of law was situated, usually on an elevated platform. When Rome embraced Christianity, the basilicas were converted into churches, the apse then being used as the seat of the bishop as well as the site of the altar.

It soon became apparent that as more and more cathedrals

Exeter: the choir-stalls and screen, separating the clergy and the laity

became regular, the tiny apse reserved for the clergy was not large enough to hold a bishop, his assistants, an altar, plus a choir of up to 50-60 monks, and so the apse was enlarged. Choirs were built westwards to accommodate the monks and leave room for the sanctuary and ambulatory, all of which we shall look at closely in a moment.

There is one more crucial historical division inside the cathedral (or church) to be understood. In medieval times the choir screen was both a physical as well as a spiritual barrier between the clergy in the east end and the laity in the west. The dramatic impact of the complete separation of the clergy from the laity and consequently the east from the west within a medieval cathedral cannot be over-emphasised. It is only when we grasp this fundamental division that the true atmosphere of the interior comes to life. The physical

Exeter: looking through the choir screen to the eastern end

expression of this partition is still there for us to see in many cathedrals and churches in the wonderful stone or timber screens that stretch right across the width of the choir.

Every cathedral originally had a rood or choir screen. They ranged from the simple and effective to a zenith of grandeur and design, such as at York Minster with its lines of saints carved in stone. The screen could be placed either across the end of the nave or at the end of the crossing, the arrangement varying from place to place. A rood is an Anglo-Saxon word meaning a cross or a crucifix. It was usual for the original screens to have a large crucifix suspended above them, with figures of the Blessed Virgin and St John to either side. If these were present, then the screen was known as a rood screen; if there were no figures, then it was called the choir screen. There was a doorway in the middle which was opened when the Sanctus bell was heard and the priest came there to give communion to the people.

The nave was frequently used for secular purposes — it was probably the only meeting-place available in a town — as it was an enormous space, with no chairs or pews except for a few wooden benches against the walls for the sick. The floor would probably still be earth, with rushes spread on it.

Maintenance of these two areas of the cathedral was also divided; the congregation being responsible for the cost of repairs to the nave while the clergy were responsible for repairs to the eastern end. French and Latin were spoken in England until about 1350, but it would have been difficult to hear what was being chanted on the other side of the rood screen and nothing could be seen of the service. You can appreciate why medieval chroniclers often referred to the congregation as being noisy and boisterous with trading being carried on, and frequent fighting. The priests of the cathedral, especially if they were monks, would take no notice of the worldly activities going on in the nave — except perhaps to complain of the noise. We shall see later how the living and sleeping quarters of the monks were directly connected to the eastern part of the cathedral which enabled their monastic routine to continue day and night.

Often there was a gallery or loft that ran across the top of the screen, from where the clergy could address or preach to the laity in the nave. Its principal function was to provide accommodation for a choir, for musicians, or occasionally in later times for an organ. Most have now disappeared, but their former presence can still be discerned in many churches by the existence of the staircase that used to lead to the gallery: this will be found built into the wall at the side of the church. The gallery was originally called a *pulpitum*, from the Latin word meaning a raised platform.

After the Reformation, when the 'mysteries' of the Roman Catholic Church were not compatible with the zeal and openness of the new Protestant religion, many of these screens were torn down. At the same time sermons became more popular, and the pulpit we are familiar with today became a separate entity and was placed in the nave to be accessible to the congregation.

Now we can make our way through the rood or choir screen and enter the eastern end of the church. First we come to the choir. The choir is always elevated higher than the nave, sometimes only by one or two steps, but often by many more. This symbolically marked the passage from the secular nave into a higher and more holy place. Here at Wells we are left in little doubt that we have left the realm of the stone-mason and entered that of the carpenter, for we are surrounded by wooden stalls, surmounted by ornate canopies and sumptuous panelling which portray the summit of craftsmanship in wood.

The choir accommodated the resident clergy who stood in their individual stalls praying and chanting the almost continual worship that went on in cathedrals in the Middle Ages. It takes little imagination for us today to stand in the centre of this elaborately-carved enclosure and breathe in the atmosphere that emanates from all the centuries of song and worship that have taken place here.

The long services required the clergy to stand for many hours, but for the elderly or infirm help was nearby in the form of misericords (from the Latin word for mercy). These were ledges on the underside of the hinged seats of the stalls which when turned up gave support to the monks or priests who could prop themselves up and sit in a standing position. They are normally hidden away under the seats of the stalls, but are well worth seeking out for the interesting carvings in which the local wood-carver often expressed his sense of humour.

At the end of the choir, and usually slightly apart from it, we find the bishop's throne, or, as we saw earlier, his 'cathedra'. Since a bishop was always accompanied by two chaplains, additional seating was provided for them, one on each side of the throne. All cathedra differ greatly in their design. Some are plain and simple, such as the throne known as St Augustine's Chair at Canterbury which is made of

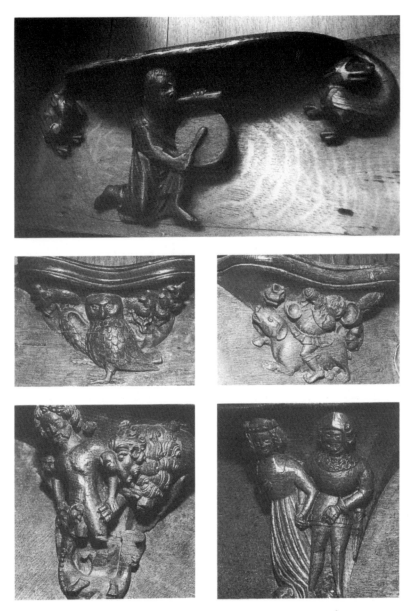

Misericord carvings: top Exeter, the others are at Norwich

Exeter: the Bishop's Throne in the choir, carved oak, 1313-16

simple slabs of Purbeck marble, or the one at Hereford which is of wood and stone. The most spectacular and literally overwhelming wooden throne is that of Exeter which towers to a height of 57 feet, of which almost every inch is festooned with carved ornament.

Beyond the choir is the area known as the presbytery, from a Greek word meaning 'the place of the elders or priests'. Here we find the most sacred part of the cathedral, the high altar, and its surrounding area known as the sanctuary. The high altar in a cathedral is always free-standing, unlike in a parish church where it is placed against a wall. The high altar was designed so that it could be sprinkled with holy water and blessed with incense from all sides. It was also raised higher than the presbytery, usually by one or two steps, again to emphasise its ultimate importance. It was because of this great importance that the high altar became a favourite target of the Puritans during the Civil War of the 17th century – if it had survived the zeal of the Reformation in the previous century. The original altars were replaced by wooden communion tables, since in the mind of the Protestants altars were associated with 'sacrifice'. Although stone altars were later allowed back, there is still a reminder of the reformers' zeal in that the word 'altar' does not appear in the Book of Common Prayer of the Anglican Church to this day.

Underneath the presbytery and choir, we find the sometimes forgotten and least understood part of a cathedral, even though it is often the most atmospheric of all – the crypt. The word 'crypt' is derived from the Greek *krupto* meaning 'to bury', and its origin leads us back to the underground catacombs of Rome and the beginnings of Christianity itself. The bodies of the early Christians had to be buried outside the city walls in the underground labyrinths of the catacombs. Later, when Rome became Christian, the first basilica churches were erected over the tombs of the martyrs (St Peter's being the most famous example), with the altar being placed closest to the exact position of the burial.

In the early centuries of the Christian Church, many people made the long journey to these burial sites in Rome and the Holy Land in the belief that by doing so the saints and martyrs would intercede on their behalf. Soon it was believed that relics alone – some part of the bodies such as a bone, or merely something that was purported to have been in their possession – had the same beneficial effect. These remains of martyrs and saints became an essential trade in the early

Worcester Cathedral crypt, 11th century

Church, and the exhumation and distribution of relics to the northern countries was extremely lucrative.

English cathedrals, as well as many other churches, acquired relics of their own, some obtained from lands afar, others the relics of a local martyr. These were placed in 'tombs' in the crypt, directly under the high altar. These relics attracted many pilgrims to visit, especially in the hope that contact with them would provide miraculous cures for various ailments. And when such a miraculous cure was reported at a particular place, it became fashionable for pilgrims to throng there by the hundred and thousand. Since every pilgrim brought an offering or gift, thereby generating the vital funds needed to help finance the running of the existing cathedral as well as future re-building, the priests in charge took great care to encourage as many as possible to visit the particular relics displayed in their crypt.

Gloucester Cathedral crypt, 11th century

In order to get thousands of pilgrims in and out of these tiny subterranean spaces, the crypts were designed with two staircases, for descending on one side and ascending on the other, and a semi-circular walkway was added which led the visitors around the outside of the tomb offering a view through three openings into the sacred site containing the relics. This was the perfect one-way system, down, around, and then up again, leaving their offerings to swell the ever-waiting coffers of the cathedral. Good examples can still be seen at Winchester, Gloucester, Rochester, York and Worcester. By far the richest and best example is to be found at Canterbury Cathedral where the space underneath became so large that it developed into a separate church in its own right, and is now the largest Norman crypt in the world. The whole of this area under the church was called the undercroft.

The clergy of these early churches soon realised that the dark, damp and cramped surroundings of the crypt were less than suitable for the display of their most treasured possessions – and hence the encouragement of the lucrative pilgrims. They followed the example of their neighbours, the French, and brought the relics up to ground-floor level and placed them in a *feretory*, or saint's chapel. The position of the feretory was usually just behind the high altar, but this can vary depending on the space available in individual cathedrals. The first feretory to appear in England was at Canterbury in 1220. This held the remains of St Thomas à Becket, murdered in the cathedral in 1170, which had originally been buried in the crypt. Others followed: Winchester and St Swithun, Ely and St Etheldreda, Durham and St Cuthbert, Westminster and St Edward, and Lincoln and St Hugh.

WE HAVE NOW REACHED the final eastern end wall or ending, which at Wells is the lady chapel. There are many patterns that can be followed to form the closure of the church, but generally there are three main types. The most common ending is a flat wall containing a massive stained-glass window of varying degrees of colour, splendour and decoration. The next is a lady chapel (dedicated to Our Lady) which is usually either polygonal or circular in shape, and again highly decorated with multi-coloured stained-glass windows. The third and rarest form of ending is the semi-circular apse, a type that is both simpler and more ancient in origin than the others but infinitely more interesting. One of the grandest examples is at Norwich Cathedral. The apse combined with the ambulatory are steeped in history and provide a fascinating link to the early Christians. The word 'ambulatory' is taken directly from the Latin and means a place for walking. And that is exactly what it is – a passage-way that runs around the whole of the outside of the choir and apse behind the high altar.

The one-way system that had worked so well for viewing the relics in the crypt was simply transferred above ground. From this

Norwich: the ambulatory curves to the left following the shape of the apse. In the centre is the entrance to one of the three chapels

walkway we can look through the openings in the apse wall into the sanctuary, just as we would have done in the crypt, but now there is much more space and light — and more space meant more pilgrims.

At Norwich Cathedral there are three chapels radiating outwards from the curving ambulatory. There is nothing particularly special about what is contained within them: in fact they are like most other chapels to be found in any cathedral throughout the country, except for one small detail. Their position on the curve of the ambulatory is symbolic, and again leads us back to the catacombs of Rome.

THE EASTERN END

Then the sepulchre chamber containing the saint's relics frequently had several more tomb recesses hewn into the walls surrounding it, to hold the remains of close followers. When the relics of saints and martyrs were subsequently transferred into churches, first into the crypt and then into the feretory, the same pattern of burial was used. Thus semi-circular tombs were carved into the wall of the apse for those clergy who wished to be buried closest to the relics. Two of these chapels at Norwich Cathedral show the same semi-circular shape, their individual altars specifically arranged so that they face due east to their spiritual home. The third is used as a lady chapel. Few people today, whether they be clergy or lay-person, give more than a passing glance to these chapels, but their shape, position and history links us with the birth of Christianity.

Now it is time to go outside, walk away from the building and turn to look at the overall structure.

THE EXTERIOR

The West Front Façade

MEMBERS OF THE PUBLIC, whether coming to attend a service or as a pilgrim, would enter the building at the western end and so here we find the most highly decorated part of the exterior. Richly ornate carving and painted sculptured figures were placed here to impress visitors. There are many west fronts in England that have become works of art in their own right. The mighty Romanesque frieze that stretches right across the front at Lincoln Cathedral (built before 1092) is the best example we have of Norman sculpture at this time.

Here at Wells we find what is regarded as the most harmonious and beautiful of all west front façades. It was designed and built by Adam Lock, one of the few early master-masons whose name has been passed down to us. Building began in 1220 in a pure Early

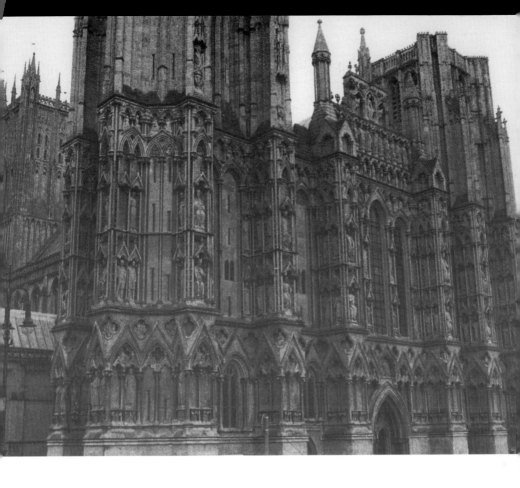

Wells Cathedral: the magnificent west front façade

English Gothic design. The front contains eighty full-sized sculptured figures that would originally have been painted in vivid primary colours. Today we can only stand and gaze at these stone figures while trying to imagine the impact those colours would have had on our senses. Not all fronts were so grand; but you'll find these entrances are usually the most impressive part of the outside of a cathedral.

Spires

THE GREATEST EXPRESSION left to us today of the incredible confidence the master-masons possessed is the spire rising from the top of the central tower.

We have seen how the whole thrust of the new Gothic design was to build higher and higher, literally reaching up to God, and the spire was the crowning glory of this belief. Spires have been painted by artists, captured in verse by poets and likened to a finger pointing to heaven. They are also landmarks to locate the cathedral which can be seen from a great distance.

The risks involved in building a spire are many and perilous, and as I was personally involved in the recent restoration of Salisbury Cathedral's 404-foot spire I can assure you that spire building is not for the faint-hearted, and my respect for the masons who built them is immense.

A spire is a way of raising a body of stone to its safest and highest point. Built on the principle of the triangle, its shape is deter-mined first and foremost by the need to reduce the mass and quantity of stone as it climbs. The higher you go so the shape and quantity of stone diminishes. This reduces wind resistance which is a major factor to add to the calculations. The three finest spires to be seen today on cathedrals in England are Chichester, Norwich and Salisbury.

Buttresses

HOT ON THE HEELS of the pointed arch and ribbed vaulting for the prize of technological advance of medieval construction was the flying buttress, or the flyer. It was invented to solve the problem brought about by ribbed vaulting. This was how to stop the upper part of the nave walls from cracking, which caused the stone vaulted roof to fall down. This disaster, often resulting in many deaths,

Sherborne Abbey: the flying buttress system, showing the flyers with counter-balancing pinnacles and lower buttresses to transfer weight to the foundations

happened with alarming regularity in the early years of ribbed vaulting. In the quest for higher, lighter and more slender stonework, the clerestory and triforium levels had become weak points. Many a weary master-mason must have scratched his head over this, saying three cantations of the Holy Rosary, and a special prayer to St Jude.

In fact, the problem they were up against was that of lateral thrust (sideways push). This sounds very complicated and technical, but actually is quite easy to understand. Basically it meant that at the point from which the vaulting ribs were sprung on the inside of the building — the triforium or clerestory level — there was a tremendous force pushing outwards against the walls, but there was nothing on the outside to counterbalance this push.

So what was the answer and how was it found? There was much travelling of master-masons between cathedrals to discuss and learn from each other how to solve this imbalance in the support system. The solution didn't come in a blinding flash of inspiration, but half the problem had already been solved centuries earlier, and was there staring them in the face lower down the walls — buttresses.

These buttresses were built against the base of the outside walls and were too short and inadequate to provide the support at the place it was needed most, the clerestory wall. We saw earlier on the inside of the building where the high vault was sprung from, but here on the outside the corresponding view is hidden from us. Nevertheless we can tell where it is by looking at where the flyer meets the clerestory wall. This point is exactly where the support is needed, and by extending the short buttress to the right height, there is now a continuous support system from the high vault, through the clerestory wall, along the flyer, and down the extended buttress to the ground foundations. With the lateral thrust now being transferred through this web of supports it meant that the walls of the nave and the high vault could become higher and higher. In small churches or abbeys it soon became a straightforward task to perform, but if we look at one of the tallest and grandest of our buildings, Westminster Abbey, then we can see how the system can be adapted and applied to accommodate such a complex structure by creating a network of intricate flyers at different levels.

When flyers were first used they were rather heavy and solid looking. This is not surprising, for after years of cracking walls and collapsing roofs, the master-masons were in no mood to under-estimate or underdesign their new solution. But soon it was realised that the flyers could be lightened and decorated to improve their appearance.

One more thing to notice about this system of flying buttresses is the pinnacle that sits on top of the upright part of the buttress. They are often pretty, some being quite delightful in their own right, but they have been put there for a specific purpose, one that is essential to the role of the buttress, that is to act as a counterbalance for the outward thrust that is at work at this point. The height of the pinnacles above the marriage of the two parts of the buttress, the flyer and the upright, was carefully calculated to act as a counter-force.

Although the whole flying buttress system is usually high up, it is worth spending some time looking at how it is put together. Is it light or heavy? Where exactly does the flyer meet the nave wall? If you are in doubt, go back inside and check, using the clerestory windows as a guide. If you see flying buttresses on the outside as you first approach the building, then you can be certain that there will be a stone-vaulted roof to the nave. No flying buttresses and you will probably see a wooden roof.

GOTHIC IN THREE STAGES

WE HAVE SEEN how the Norman style evolved into the Gothic style primarily as a consequence of the invention of the point-ed arch. This new Gothic style was to dominate from 1150 until about 1650, a time span of nearly five centuries. However, as we have already seen in the history of vaulting, there was a continuous and sometimes radical development of the Gothic style continually at work. Therefore a church built in 1150 would be very different from one built in 1320, and that in turn would differ from one built in 1600, although all three can be described as 'Gothic'. The Gothic period is therefore normally split into three distinct sub-divisions, together with a rough estimate of their dates and the developments they contain.

Don't be put off by this. I suggest you choose one thing in a church that particularly strikes a chord with you. It could be a particular shape or a form that delights, intrigues, or arouses your curiosity. Then find out from which period this has come. Repeat this on different visits to churches. In this way you can slowly build up your own collection of personal favourites to which you can add stage by stage. Before you know where you are you will find that you have learned the different styles with no effort.

It is worth remembering before we look at the details of these three periods of the Gothic style that it was only as recently as Victorian times that these periods were actually classified in this way. They should therefore only be used as rough guidelines and no more. The medieval stone-masons didn't wake up one morning and decide that they were going to use a completely new style. There were always prolonged transitional periods and overlap from one style to the next, reflecting some stone-masons being adventurous and trying out new ideas, while others preferred to continue using older tried-and-tested techniques. As a craftsman, I must admit that I have no great friend-ship with these strict lines of demarcation, but as this has now become the accepted language which is most used in guide books I have to bend before the wind.

The names of these three sub-divisions of the Gothic period together with their generally-accepted dates are:

Early English 1150-1270

Decorated 1270-1370

Perpendicular 1370-1650

Wells: gable end, a favourite Early English arrangement
of lancet windows and arches

Early English Period (1150-1270)

As this first stage of the new Gothic style emerged from the preceding heavy Norman work, we would expect to find a fresh simplicity about the details. And this is exactly what we do find.

The tall, long, elongated 'lancet' window is the hallmark of Early English. These lancet windows were mostly arranged in groups of two, three, five or seven, often surmounted by a Gothic arch and the trefoils, quatrefoils and cinquefoils which were a major design form during this time. They remained the dominant decorative theme throughout the whole of the Gothic period, used everywhere on the fabric of the building both inside and out. Circular windows (often called 'rose windows') were also frequently used, especially placed above a group of lancets to make a favourite and distinctive combination typical of this period.

Wells: an Early English pointed arch inset with the typical 'ogee' shape from the Decorated period

Two of our major cathedrals – Wells and Salisbury – were built almost completely during this Early English period. (The tower and spire of Salisbury were added a century later.)

Exeter: the tracery of a Decorated window

Decorated Period (1270-1370)

THE WINDOWS ONCE AGAIN carry the major characteristic feature of this period. But instead of it being the shape of the windows themselves, now it is the stone geometric decoration within the window or 'tracery'. In the previous Early English style there were tentative early attempts at 'tracery' decoration but they were simple forms such as one quatrefoil. Now they have developed into complex geometric and elaborate flowing designs. These windows standing on narrow mullions became one of the most expressive places for the art of the stone-mason to delight and dazzle the observer.

This is the period when niches were set into the walls of the tower, buttresses and west fronts, shaped to contain statues of saints, apostles and other religious figures. Most of these niches remain but

Wells: the contrasting styles of a Perpendicular window on the left and Decorated on the right

many of the statues they once contained were removed, smashed or defaced either at the time of the Reformation or by the Puritans.

The best examples of the Decorated period are to be found in the nave of York Minster, the nave and transepts of Exeter Cathedral, and the lady chapel and central lantern at Ely Cathedral.

Perpendicular Period (1370-1650)

THERE WAS NOW a more abrupt change to simpler straight lines. The new style Perpendicular windows had several advantages: they let

Opposite: *Winchester — west window, the tall Perpendicular mullions supported by transoms*

GOTHIC IN THREE STAGES

the maximum of light through; they enabled windows of a vast size to be built, especially dramatic east windows behind the altar; and they also gave much more scope to the glass painter whose skill at creating stained glass was now reaching its peak.

The vertical bars of stone continued in straight lines from top to bottom of the window, and it is these mullions that gave the name 'Perpendicular' to this period. They provided more strength than the flowing designs of the Decorated period but their great heights meant that they in turn had to be supported in order to stop them bulging. This was achieved with horizontal bars of stone, called 'transoms', that were put in the lower part of the large windows.

The shape of the arch also changed significantly during this period, and gave us the distinctive 'four-centred' arch, commonly known as the 'Tudor' arch. 'Four-centred' simply means that each arch is comprised of four different curves, two on each side.

Fan-vaulting reached its ultimate convoluted beauty during this time, and panelling also played a large part in the perpendicular combinations found inside and outside, usually containing bands of quatrefoils for decoration.

One of the first and finest examples of the Perpendicular period is to be found at Gloucester Cathedral in the choir and transepts. This new style soon spread throughout the country, and was dominant in all churches built in the next two and a half centuries, from East Anglia to the West Country.

Perpendicular details, especially the four-centred arch and the square-headed doorway, transferred themselves into nearly every type of building in England at this time. They appeared in houses, castles, barns and even cottages, but special mention has to be made of the colleges of the universities of Oxford and Cambridge, which immersed themselves in the Perpendicular style. The masterpiece is the Chapel of King's College, Cambridge which was built in 1508-15. The walls of this unique building, which appear more glass than stone, are perhaps the clearest indication of how far the abilities of

Gloucester: the fan-vaulted ceiling of the cloisters, 14th century

stone-masons had progressed from the thick and solid walls of the Norman period only a few centuries earlier.

In these Gothic churches we should remember that the invention of the pointed arch together with ribbed vaulting allowed the builders to achieve their aims of a higher thrust upwards towards Heaven, a feeling of lightness, a slender linear quality to everything, where windows replaced thick heavy walls and allowed natural light to pour into the whole church.

GUIDED BY A STONE-MASON

CHAPTER THREE

Building
a
Cathedral

How on earth did they build these medieval cathedrals? As we approach such a vast structure on foot, there are a host of questions that pass through our minds. It could be the first, the tenth, or indeed the hundredth time that we are walking towards a cathedral, but the message is always the same. Anticipation, excitement, fascination, and then questions. Who built and designed such a huge structure? How was it done? And how has it stood there for so long, in some cases for nearly a thousand years?

Understanding the ancient and mysterious craft of the stone-mason is one of the keys which can unlock the secrets of construction that lie hidden within a medieval cathedral.

THE MASTER-MASON AND HIS RESPONSIBILITIES

Today an architect is employed to design a building, and a structural engineer to calculate the stresses and strains of the materials used. Others such as the clerk of works and quantity surveyors assist with the finances and general running of the project. A thousand years ago the story was very different.

The master-mason was architect, quantity surveyor, civil engineer and artist all rolled into one. He designed the overall plan as well as the details, he chose the materials, he calculated the stresses and strains that would occur, and then he supervised the whole building project from the foundations to the top of the tower.

The master-mason was commissioned by the bishop, abbot or dean and chapter. Master-masons gained reputations for their work and travelled long distances to meet and compare techniques with other masons. No doubt there would have been competition to acquire the services of someone up-to-date and experienced. The

Previous page: *Tintern Abbey, Monmouthshire*

*A rare insight into medieval building methods from a French
miniature, 1448, 'Girart de Roussillon',
reproduced courtesy Austrian National Library, Vienna*

THE MASTER-MASON

mason would expect his sponsor to provide the initial finances to start building at the eastern end. The money could come from one source or a combination of sources. There might be a wealthy donor who on his death would be buried within the cathedral, or the bishop would raise taxes in the diocese, and there was the ever-increasing monastic wealth based on the lucrative wool trade. Once the eastern end was raised, roofed and consecrated and the relics displayed then pilgrims would provide an extra source of funds to help finance the building of the nave.

There were many craftsmen involved with building a cathedral and the master-mason was responsible for them all: the stone-masons; carpenters and joiners who were a close second in their importance to the raising of the fabric; blacksmiths who made tools for everybody and kept them sharp, as well as nails, door hinges, railings, locks and keys and decorative wrought iron; glaziers who were needed for the glasswork which increased in size as the Gothic style evolved, and the use of stained glass became an art form in its own right; plumbers who were usually found on the roofs of the cathedrals covering them with long sheets of lead; and the plasterers and painters who put the final colourful touches on the stonework.

A single master-mason took on a role that today requires at least five or six people, and he had to have a good deal of experience and expertise. One of the main reasons he was able to achieve this wealth of knowledge and the confidence to use it was because first and foremost the master-mason was a craftsman. He knew intimately the materials he was dealing with, how to utilise them to the best advantage, how they behaved under pressure, how they weathered, how they should be prepared and stored, and how to time their positioning in the structure. The architect and his entourage today all too often lack this vital organic and intimate understanding between a craftsman and his material – with depressing results.

It should not be taken as fanciful or indeed romantic to remember this vital link between a master-mason, his fellow craftsmen, and the materials that would be used to raise the structure. Wisdom, strength of character, sensitivity and dynamism are all words that could sit easily on the shoulders of the medieval master-mason. These were men who had already served a full apprenticeship before taking up the mantle of a master-mason. They could themselves carve from any size or type of stone anything from a basic plain moulding to a full-size sculpture of one of the saints or the Holy Family, or indeed any of the irreverent and fallacious figures for gargoyles, corbels or misericords. They had travelled as journeymen craftsmen throughout Britain, and probably even to the great cathedrals of France, Spain and Italy where they would have seen different solutions used to solve the problems posed by the complexity of cathedral building. This transference of knowledge wasn't learned from books. It passed from mason to mason, from city to city, from country to country across Europe. It was the vital link for the Gothic style to evolve as it rose higher and higher to peaks and heights once thought impossible. As we gaze upwards today at the spire of Salisbury Cathedral, all 404 feet stand as testimony to the belief of the master-mason in his design, his confidence in his materials, and his relationship to the craftsmen and craftswomen of the Middle Ages, who were the true creators of these magnificent cathedrals.

GUILDS

IT IS OFTEN THOUGHT that a medieval cathedral would have been built from start to finish in one uninterrupted stretch of time. In fact this was seldom the case. Continuity of work depended on many things, but the most important was the availability of funds which could easily dry up because of the tenuous nature of life and the economy in the Middle Ages. The fluctuation in the price of wool, war, famine and plague all had a significant effect on building projects – and of course on the craftsmen that carried them out. As a result of this the craft guilds and lodges became of great importance in providing help and refuge for their members in times of hard-ship.

Each individual craft had its own respective guild or lodge with strict rules about wages, holidays, apprentices, journeymen, and the amount of time worked in summer and who would be retained for work through the winter. As a result, these guilds became very tight-ly knit communities over the years as skills were passed on from father to son. The knowledge of when particular work would finish and where future work could be found was vitally important information to the crafts (an idle craftsman was also a hungry one), and as such became the origin of the mystery and secrecy that still surrounds some guilds and lodges to this day.

TRAINING THE STONE-MASON

ON DAY ONE a lad arrives to start his seven-year apprenticeship. He is tied to an older mason who is going to teach him the rudiments of the craft, and he is given his personal mason's mark which he will put on every stone he carves for the rest of his life. This mark served two purposes: a mason was paid by the number of stones he produced, and his mark was indisputable evidence of his work; and when the stones were to be fixed in a building, if they didn't match, or were the wrong size, or had been badly carved, then the master-mason knew who to talk to.

The apprentice was initially known as a 'banker mason' because he worked at a banker or bench. ('Bench' is from an Old English word and 'bank' from a Norman-French word which have a common origin as meaning a shelf.) Here the apprentice would carve the details given to him in blocks of stone which would sit on the banker. His first stones would be very plain, and he would spend the first year making square 'ashlar' blocks. These ashlar blocks are smooth-faced and finely-jointed stones used to make plain but very exact stone walls.

This task would teach the apprentice the basic skills needed for

A banker mason carving foliage

all masonry. He would learn to use a range of chisels: a 'pitcher', a 'punch', a 'claw', and a 'boaster' to create the smooth surface, and his wooden mallet, a large cone-shaped piece of timber usually made of apple-wood for suppleness and long life. He would also be taught the importance and basic use of the square and compasses for the use of setting-out and accurate measurement, which was essential on such a massive and complex building.

TRAINING THE STONE-MASON

In his second year he would be allowed to start decorating the square blocks with a variety of shapes known as mouldings. Mouldings decorated all the arches, doorways and windows, as well as many other details throughout the cathedral. The depth and shape of these mouldings can tell a trained eye roughly what date or period the doorway or window was carved.

So how did our young apprentice know what shape he had to cut the moulding? Well, he was given a precise cross-section of these sometimes complex shapes by a 'template', a thin layer of wood with the exact shape required upon it. (In later times metal was preferred for the template as it did not shrink, and zinc is used for this purpose today.) The templates were made in the template 'shop' and they were formed by the shapes passed to them by the 'tracing floor'. This is where we would find the master-mason most of the time. Here his scaled drawings and design for the cathedral would be incised in plaster, and then each elevation would be scaled up and the details and shapes needed formed into templates to be used by the masons' shop.

Geometry and draughtsmanship were very important on the tracing floor. Whole stone vaults, to be suspended high above the nave, had to be set out full size and be cut down to shape here. This is why master-masons were held in such high esteem, because it took not only great skill and an eye for beauty of design, but also much courage to conceive and push through such designs.

After three or four years at his banker the apprentice would be given a year on the tracing floor learning how to set out, draw, and finally bring to life the structural elements and designs conceived by the master-mason. The remains of two such tracing floors can still be seen today at York Minster and Wells Cathedral (the latter is not open to the public).

The last year or two of apprenticeship would be given to the carving of foliage, leaves, and possibly even figures. All these would be done free-hand without any template to work from. The apprentice's further career depended on how he fared at all of these disciplines. If he was skilled at the carving of foliage used to decorate the capitals, then he might be further apprenticed to the carving shop where eventually he would learn to make life-size statues of the saints and other dignitaries. If he showed aptitude and flair on the tracing floor then he would be groomed as a master-mason of the future, as the total mastery of geometry and all its proportions were essential for the ultimate accolade, but this would not be for many years yet.

If the lad took to neither of these highly-skilled professions then he would continue to carve his stones by the template.

His seven-year apprenticeship finished, the newly-qualified mason became known as a 'journeyman'. That is, in parallel with other time-served apprentices of different crafts, he was now qualified to work at his trade for a day's wages (*jour* being French for day). As a journeyman he therefore became a member of the large group of masons.

Within this group there were two distinct types of masons: the ones who used a mallet and chisel for carving, and those who used mortar to lay the stones in their correct positions in a building. The former group has always been considered the more skilled and has consequently always received higher wages. They were originally known as 'lathomers' but today are referred to as 'banker masons' or 'stone carvers'. The second group were originally known as 'cementarius' or 'setters' but today go by the name of 'fixers'.

While a journeyman often stayed with the master-mason under whom he had trained, there was no obligation to do so. He was free to hire himself to whomsoever he wished. Some of the more enlightened journeymen took this latter option and travelled with their tools to seek work in another area – becoming a 'journey' man in the other meaning of the word. This could mean, and frequently did, that he travelled not only the length and breadth of Britain but also abroad to France, Italy and Spain. He was not merely journeying to seek work, but to see for himself the type of building and new ideas that were going on elsewhere.

It wasn't just the stone-masons who went off on their travels, so did other craftsmen such as carpenters and smiths. It is therefore little wonder that this interchange of manpower between cathedrals and countries was one of the main reasons that the new Gothic style spread so quickly throughout Western Europe. Ideas were passed, and vital news was carried by the craftsmen about new techniques and advances from the old Romanesque to the new style of Gothic at the beginning of the 12th century.

HOW TO SET OUT AND BUILD A CATHEDRAL

THAT'S THE KIND of title which conjures up all kind of daunting questions. Let's take the monumental task and strip it down to its basics, and see if we can use what we know already and add some extra and crucial medieval working methods, and then bring them all together in order to build our cathedral.

Once the site for the new cathedral has been chosen, and before any but the crudest of outline plans are drawn, there is one very important thing to be done. The lime pits must be dug at the site at least six months before a stone is laid.

Let's imagine that we are the master-mason. Therefore we are the architect, engineer, craftsman and artist, all rolled into one. The plans for the cathedral would be drawn and set in plaster. A scale model in wood would be made of the overall design, to give a 3-dimensional image of the whole building.

These scaled measurements are then transferred into a full-size layout. To do this we use the following: a large square which has the Pythagorean triangle of 3,4,5, proportions to ensure true right angles: pegs and string, and the most important measuring instrument that we will use for all of the main proportions of the cathedral, a pole. This is also known as a rod or perch, and was carefully made of iron by the blacksmith. The pole is square in section, and for our cathedral it will be 16 feet long. I say that because a pole actually varied by as much as three feet in certain parts of the country, but the average was around our chosen length of 16 feet.

We can see how the pole system gave the cathedrals such a harmonic feel. From the outside wall to the middle of the aisle pier is one pole, the nave is two poles wide, and the other aisle is of course one pole in width. This means that the whole building is four poles wide. The bays (pier to pier) that reach all the way up the nave are also one pole in width and because they are also one pole in height they are square in dimension. The presbytery is four poles long, and the nave and crossing eight, so that makes the whole cathedral twelve poles in length.

The height of the nave to the roof level will be six poles, while at the nave arcade there will be three poles to the tops of the arches, one for the triforium, and two for the clerestory.

Remember how the orientation of the cathedral is on an east-to-west axis, commonly based on where the sun rose in the east on the day attributed to the saint to whom the building was dedicated. Once this has been determined by the rising and setting of the sun (aided by a magnetic lode-stone, the forerunner of a compass), it is time to start pegging out the plan of the building on the ground. As soon as the master-mason is satisfied with the pegged lay-out, the foundations will be dug and filled with the correct material. The lack of good solid and deep enough foundation with the correct infill plagued many of the early cathedral builders. This usually resulted in the central tower cracking, sinking or collapsing.

A suitable quarry in the vicinity of the building would almost certainly have been chosen at an early stage, and also a nearby forest to provide all the timber used in the construction. In the absence of a suitable quarry, arrangements would have been made to bring the stones by water, for example, from a far-away quarry, perhaps in Normandy, and in this case the stones would be cut to size before shipping. The master-mason would now revisit the quarry to select exactly which type and quality of stone was to be used, and at what cost. The 'bedding plane' (how a stone is laid down and formed) along with its quality and accessibility, are all questions that had to be resolved here.

THE MAGIC OF LIME MORTAR

THE LIME PITS at the cathedral site contained quicklime or 'burnt lime'. When water was added to it it would boil and burn until it turned into 'lime putty' with a smooth cream-cheese texture. After six months in the pits, covered over and protected from frosts and rain, the lime putty is at its best working texture. It is dug out of the ground and sand added to it in a 1:1 ratio. This is now called 'lime mortar' and would be used as the bedding material between all the stones. No cement as we know it today was used and that is one of the main reasons why these medieval buildings are still standing. Lime mortar, because it is a soft, porous and malleable material, helps the building to move and even crack without major damage. It acts like a cushion to every jointed stone and helps the structure breathe. Whereas modern cement, used extensively by the Victorian restorers and still unfortunately today, performs the opposite function, because of its brittle nature it actually strangles the building and speeds up dramatically the decay of all historic buildings.

The medieval builders knew only too well the magic properties of lime, and eulogised their reverence of it like this:

The French say 'Lime at a hundred years is still but a child'.
The Scots say 'When a hundred years have been and gone,
    then shall good mortar harden like stone'.
The Turks say 'Look after me for a year, and I shall look after
    your children for a thousand'.

As we have seen, the cathedral was almost always built starting at the presbytery and choir. In this way the east end of the building would be completed first and the high altar could be consecrated as soon as possible. This provided an enclosed space for the priests to hold their services, and for the display of relics to attract pilgrims whose donations helped to provide money for the building fund.

As the cathedral steadily rose upwards the master-mason had to decide what type of lifting gear and scaffold would be used. The scaffold would be made of wood poles lashed together with strong cord, and the lifting gear consisted of the simple but very effective use of pulleys, winches and windlasses, constructed and placed at the most strategic and easily accessible parts of the building.

This was where the master-mason really earned his corn, because forethought and ingenious planning at this stage would save time and money, both crucial to the ever-watchful eye of a prior or bishop. Scaffolding could be tied into, or suspended from, the ever-rising masonry walls and towers, but it needed the perceptive eye and mind of the master-mason to envisage this in advance. One of many things a master-mason might attend to during the course of the day was how to raise 2-ton blocks of stone or 60-feet long oak beams to the top of a roof 200 feet high exactly where and when they were needed, with the correct preparatory work down on the ground.

He worried whether the arches in the high vault had been set out correctly. They had been spot-on when laid out on the tracing floor, but had that accuracy been transferred 200 feet up in the air when having to move 2-ton blocks of stone would prove difficult? Was the lime mortar of consistent strength, or were the mortar-workers cheating him, or too lazy to check, or both? A newly-arrived journeyman from the great abbey of St-Denis in Paris had warned him that the flying buttresses looked too heavy, and may actually push in the tops of the nave walls instead of steadying them. All these matters had to be dealt with.

The mighty soaring Gothic cathedrals we see today are the successes of an evolutionary style which strove to produce the tallest possible church and so literally reach up towards heaven. This ambition created a myriad of constructional problems never before encountered and many were the failures along the way.

CHAPTER FOUR

The
Stones
of Britain

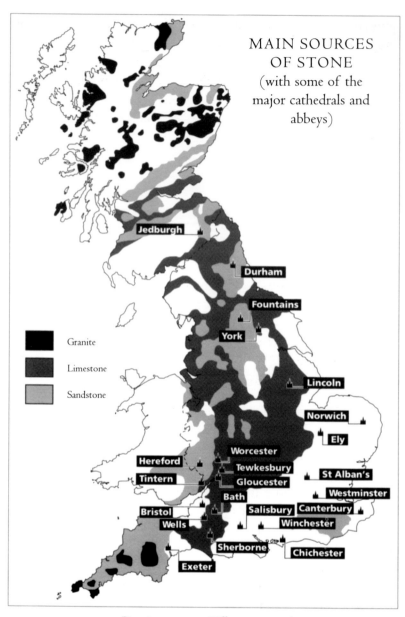

MAIN SOURCES
OF STONE
(with some of the
major cathedrals and
abbeys)

Jedburgh

Durham

Fountains

York

Granite

Limestone

Sandstone

Lincoln

Norwich

Ely

Worcester

Hereford

Tewkesbury

Tintern

Gloucester

St Alban's

Bath

Westminster

Bristol

Salisbury   Canterbury

Wells

Winchester

Sherborne

Chichester

Exeter

Previous page: *Wells, nave capital*

THE STONES OF BRITAIN

STONE IS THE MAIN MATERIAL of construction in almost all of Britain's cathedrals, abbeys and churches. It is a fascinating and beautiful material that is little understood by most people outside the specialised craft of the stone-mason or the academic world of the geologist. There are three main questions that are asked time and time again by a lay-person who comes across a stone building and instinctively and enthusiastically wants to know more. They are:

What is it made of?
Why is it that colour?
and What is it called?

The good news is that you don't have to be a geologist to understand the answer to these questions. If you follow this step-by-step guide of how to identify a stone with me, then you can start to notice and understand the stones that surround you whichever part of the country you are in.

Stones are divided into two main categories: limestones and sandstones. So the first and most important distinction we have to make with our stone is simply to decide whether it is a limestone or a sandstone.

LIMESTONE

BY LOOKING AT THE MAP we can see that there is a broad sweeping area stretching from Dorset in the south up through the Midlands and into Yorkshire in the north. This area contains the bulk of Britain's limestone and is known as 'the limestone belt'. In medieval times transferring stone from one place to another had to be kept to an absolute minimum due to the difficulty and cost of transport. So as a rule-of-thumb guide almost all of the stone buildings found inside or around this 'limestone belt' we can assume are made of limestone.

What is it made of?

SEDIMENTARY LIMESTONE. Quite simply it means that this is the way in which the stone was formed or laid down as sediment at the bottom of the sea. It is always in layer upon layer – not always visible to the naked eye – like slices of pasta in a lasagne.

CALCIUM CARBONATE (LIME). This is what is in the sediment that is laid down. It is the same substance which forms the bones of our skeletons as well as the shells of snails and numerous other sea creatures. It is this self-same calcium carbonate from the remains of sea creatures that died millions of years ago and formed a sediment which now reappears as limestone. The binding material holding all these limestones together is liquefied calcium carbonate.

OOLITES. It's a shame that with such an interesting name these oolites are barely visible to the naked eye. They are tiny grains of calcium carbonate that have been rolled over and over on the sea bed in shallow water. You may hear a stone referred to as 'oolitic limestone'. All this means is that it has a high percentage of oolites, some of which may be seen by the naked eye.

THE BEDDING PLANE OF A STONE

THE LAYERS OF SEDIMENT, consisting of calcium carbonate, whole shells, and oolites, are sometimes very easy to define, but frequently they are not. It is absolutely crucial for a stone-mason to determine this before he starts to carve his stone. It is known as 'the bedding plane' or simply 'the bed'. The position in which a stone is laid in a building is always related to the way in which its 'bed' runs, and there are three such positions.

NATURAL BEDDED. As its name suggests, this is the way in which

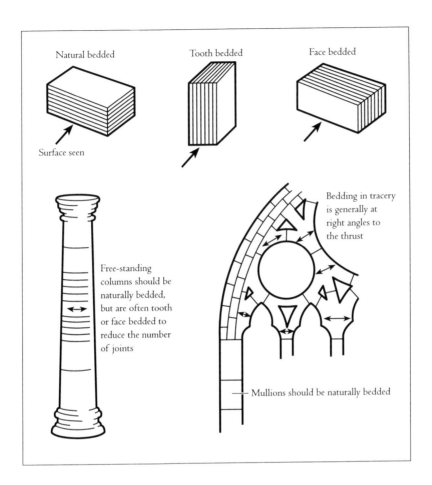

Natural bedded

Surface seen

Tooth bedded

Face bedded

Free-standing
columns should be
naturally bedded,
but are often tooth
or face bedded to
reduce the number
of joints

Bedding in tracery
is generally at
right angles to
the thrust

Mullions should be naturally bedded

the stone was originally laid down – horizontally, like layers of pasta. This is the most commonly-used type of bedding plane in a building, and almost all walls would be built using a natural bed.

TOOTH OR TEETH BEDDED. If we now turn the bed upwards on one end (so that the pasta layers are vertical), we have a stone that is said to be tooth bedded. The analogy with a set of teeth is obvious. Stones laid in this way are used for details such as arches and cornices.

FACE BEDDED. This is where the stone is turned once more so that instead of the ends of the layers visible to us, we now have the whole of the 'pasta sheet' with its length and height facing us. In other words, one flat face with no ends visible at all. As a general rule, it is very bad masonry practice to face bed stones, and it should only rarely be done on special details. The reason for this is that as the stone weathers, the slices of 'pasta' will simply fall off the face, peeling away in the layers in which it was laid down.

Why is it that colour?

THE COLOUR OF STONES can confuse people even more than the composition, which isn't surprising considering they cover such a wide colour spectrum. You'll find limestones in pure white, grey, buff, blue, red, yellow, orange and brown, and indeed some colours that we can't even find a name to describe. The colour is mostly formed by one ingredient, iron oxide. This comes from impurities that occur quite naturally in the stone and gives it a distinctive colour character.

What is it called?

THESE ARE THE NAMES of the most commonly-used limestones, their colours, and where they can be seen around the country.

PORTLAND STONE

IT IS FASCINATING to realise that a huge part of the Dorset coast-line is piled up majestically in central London. Portland stone has been used for many notable buildings in the city, including Whitehall, the Palace of Westminster and the British Museum. Sir Christopher Wren was the first to commission its use on a grand scale and he frequently visited the Isle of Portland so he could choose the stone personally. He shipped over a million tons of it around the south-east coast and up the river Thames to rebuild St Paul's and other churches after the Great Fire of 1666.

Portland stone is white, and closer inspection reveals that it is composed of layers of tiny shells. If you get into the habit of looking extremely closely at materials such as stone, possibly carrying a magnifying glass with you when you go out looking at buildings, you'll discover a whole new world. These layers of shells in Portland stone tell us two things. First that it is a limestone. Second, and more importantly, it is the key to telling the quarryman and later the stonemason in which 'bedding plane' the stone has been formed or laid down, and hence which way it should be cut and then placed in the building.

The composition of Portland stone is very compact, pure and true. This makes it especially good for carving as well as any kind of building work. Not without reason it is known throughout the craft as Britain's finest limestone.

BATH STONE

AS ITS NAME SUGGESTS, this stone is found in the area surrounding Bath, and most of the city's buildings – Roman, medieval and Georgian – are built with it. It comes from four main quarries, Monk's Park, Limpey Stoke, Combe Down and Westwood. Bath stone is a warm, yellow or buff coloured, oolitic limestone. Close inspection also reveals the small shells that tell us its sedimentary bedding plane.

COTSWOLD STONE

GUITING STONE from near Cheltenham in Gloucestershire is mainly responsible for giving the Cotswolds its delicious, warm, golden glow. There are also many small local quarries and even farms where stone was, and still is, easily accessible and cheap to transport. It is fairly soft though. This is due to the iron oxide impurities which are responsible for its lovely colour but make it less good for a permanent building material. It is particularly attractive in the dry-stone walls in the area.

Ham Hill Stone

Anyone who has travelled through Somerset and Dorset will know this tawny ochre-coloured limestone. It shows us its sedimentary bed plane extremely clearly, due to clay and shells being laid down amongst the limestone, forming a fascinating sight wherever it is used. Although it is beautiful aesthetically, it is a stone-mason's nightmare to carve because it is so soft and full of impurities. The large stones can actually fall into two parts when being worked, due to the presence of a soft clay strip concealed within. It is just as if every tenth layer of good healthy hard pasta in the lasagne has been replaced by a layer of soft cream. You can see Ham Stone, from Ham Hill in Somerset, in all its flawed splendour at Sherborne Abbey, Montacute House, and hundreds of churches and market squares around the area.

Ketton Stone

Richly golden brown in colour, Ketton stone from near Stamford in Lincolnshire is known as 'King of the Oolites' because it is a pure oolitic limestone without any shells in its constitution. This stone is much used in the Cambridge area, where most of the older buildings in the city are constructed with it. I was introduced to it during restoration work on King's College and Trinity College, Cambridge, when I found it to be a lovely stone to carve, and very 'forgiving' in its texture – that means that it 'knits' together well when restoring a small indent or piece of a large detail.

Other notable limestones, both creamy white in colour, are Ancaster from near Grantham in Lincolnshire and Clipsham from Leicestershire, which are used throughout the Midlands.

SANDSTONE

BRITAIN CONTAINS three main areas of sandstone: the Weald of Sussex; the Forest of Dean extending into South Wales; and a long, broad sweeping band stretching from Cheshire through Lancashire, Yorkshire and Scotland right up to Caithness in the far north.

So what is the difference between a sandstone and a limestone? Although they are both sedimentary rocks (laid down under water in layer after layer), they are very different in their composition. Whereas limestone is made of calcium carbonate (remains of sea creatures), sandstone is made up of three main minerals.

The first and most important is quartz, then comes feldspar, and finally mica. Let's look more closely at quartz, because it is our key to understanding how and why sandstone was formed. We can see quartz very clearly in most sandstones. It is the tiny sparkly particles that glint, and give the impression of glass fragments. Granite and other igneous (fire-formed) rocks are made of quartz and are the parents of sandstone. Little specks of quartz were washed away from the igneous rocks, and together with mica and feldspar were laid down as sediment to form sandstone. So we can refer to sandstone as 'a child of the volcanoes'.

You would expect sandstone to be durable, coming from such tough and gritty parents as granite. Generally it is, but it depends on the material binding the particles together. (If you imagine a good sauce for spaghetti containing minced meat, chopped vegetables and herbs and the binding material is the tomato sauce that holds them together, then these ingredients represent the particles of quartz, mica and feldspar.) Whereas in limestone the binding material for the shells and oolites is always liquefied calcium carbonate, in sandstone it can be one of several things. The most common is also the most durable and hence the most widely found – silica.

The bedding plane of sandstone is similar to that already described for limestone. Here are the names of some of the best and most widely used sandstones, what they look like, and where they can be found.

HOLLINGTON STONE

THIS SANDSTONE is found and used throughout the Midlands and the north of England. Its colour ranges from salmon through pink to red. Its use can clearly be seen in the cathedrals at Hereford, Worcester, Birmingham, Coventry and Lichfield. There is also a cream-coloured variety of this sandstone and this can be seen at its best in Covent Garden, London, where it is used for the colonnades and balustrades.

WEALDON STONE

THIS IS A FINE-GRAINED yellowish sandstone but with brown veins running through it, caused by plant debris being left behind when the sediment was laid down. This little pocket of sandstone in Sussex is tucked away in the middle of a limestone area. It is therefore a 'good one' to go and find if you are ever in the district. It can be seen best at the following places: the Elizabethan house of Wakehurst Place; Bodiam Castle; Baynham and Battle Abbeys; the Saxon church at Worth; Rudyard Kipling's house at Burwash; the Italian Gardens at Hever Castle.

West Yorkshire Sandstone

THE LARGEST CONCENTRATION of active sandstone quarries in Britain are to be found in West Yorkshire. At present there are over twenty, mainly supplying the durable paving stones known as 'millstone grit'. 'Bramley Fall' is a famous example, used on many engineering projects such as the lining of dock walls and for the Euston Arch in London (criminally demolished in 1962). Yorkshire 'gritstone' paving is found throughout London and the City of Westminster which still specifies its use. You can walk on it yourself at any of these major London sites: Bank of England, Woolwich Arsenal, Royal Festival Hall, Old Bailey and Covent Garden.

Stainton Stone

THE SANDSTONE from Stainton, Co. Durham is now used in Edinburgh as a substitute for Craigleith stone, the original stone of which Edinburgh was built. Its colour is buff with brown speckles. To me, Edinburgh has always been the 'Bath' of Scotland, and it is not really fair to point out any particular building. They almost all without exception have fine quality and interesting details to offer, showing these two stones at their best.

Devon Sandstone

THERE IS ONE MORE isolated pocket of sandstone that deserves a mention. Like Devon cattle this sandstone is a rich deep red in colour. Its claim to fame is not that it is the hardest, but the oldest sandstone in the country. It is used throughout Devon and Exmoor for general building but it is a poor stone for carving details. Despite that it can be found in many Devon and Somerset churchyards.

GRANITE

WHAT IS GRANITE, and where is it found? The answer to the second question is easy — Scotland and Cornwall. Granite forms the oldest part of the British Isles. It dates from the time when there were still volcanoes boiling away in this part of the world, long before the 'ordinary' limestone and sandstone were formed. Granite belongs to a group of 'igneous' rocks, from the Greek word for fire, formed when the volcanic rocks were cooling from their molten state. They cooled slowly at great depths and the solid rocks formed are known as granite. They are composed almost entirely of silica, the

same chemical substance as the quartz of sandstone, but with very different characteristics. Granite is very coarse-grained, extremely hard and very durable.

In Cornwall granite is used most impressively in local village churches and small cottages. Perhaps its most dramatic effect can be seen at Castle Drogo, Devon and Altarnun Church, Cornwall. In Scotland, many fortified castles and isolated churches are examples of the use of different coloured granites that are rich in this area.

Altarnun, Cornwall: Celtic granite cross 14 centuries old

FLINT

EAST ANGLIA is the home of flint and the almost-forgotten art of flint-knapping – the process of shaping the flint nodules into squares or other shapes for use in building work. Flints are found as isolated nodules in chalk, and because they break into sharp edges in a regular and controllable way, prehistoric man soon discovered their usefulness as tools. When cut flint is as sharp as a razor.

Flint-knapping can be done either by using a small hammer or with a tool dating from the times of Stone Age man, a deer antler. I have used both, and much prefer the latter. I was also extremely fortunate to be taught by a young flint-knapper from Swaffham in Norfolk, just down the road from Grime's Graves (now run by English Heritage and well worth a visit), where the ancient craft of

Hales Church, Norfolk, built of flint and stone

East Lexham, Norfolk: Saxon flint round tower 1,200 years old, probably the most ancient in Britain

flint-knapping is demonstrated. You'll see flint used in many buildings in East Anglia, particularly in King's Lynn and Norwich, and in hundreds of churches in the area. But why should flint be used in this region in preference to other types of stone? The reason was simply that there was no other natural source of stone there, and flint and brick were used instead. Flint is so dense and hard that it cannot absorb any water at all, making it a very durable material.

In several other parts of the country, notably Somerset, Dorset and Devon, you will frequently find something that looks identical to flint, but which is in fact called 'chert'. Although it is (geologically) slightly younger than flint itself, chert is basically the same and can be worked in a similar manner.

BRICK

THE BRICKS we use today are all of a uniform size but in medieval times there was no standardisation and they were baked in all shapes and sizes. Bricks are made by digging up a suitable clay from the earth, shaping it in a mould and then heating it to a high temperature in a kiln or oven.

As with all other materials in a medieval building, the clay would usually be extracted from the ground as close as possible to where it would be used. It is quite common for the bricks used in a rural parish church to have started life in the next field to the churchyard irrespective of the quality of the clay. As we have seen, brick was often used in parts of the country where local stone was not available, for example for parish churches in East Anglia or Kent where it was used in conjunction with flint or timber.

We have to acknowledge the Romans here and their mastery of making bricks and using them. They were often referred to as 'Roman tiles' because they were very long, wide and broad. The Romans used bricks as a construction base that was then covered over by a layer of stone, marble or plaster. Many of the tiles or bricks left by the Romans were reused by the Normans because they were made so well, and it is not unusual to find odd ones built into the walls of churches. If you find a brick between one and two feet in length it is probably Roman.

MARBLE

MARBLE IS FORMED from limestone that has been subjected to great heat or pressure, or both. The fossils or sea shell deposits then disappear and are replaced by crystals. Broadly speaking, there is no 'true' marble found in the British Isles, although there are three tiny pockets of marble on the islands of Iona and Skye in Scotland, and at County Galway in Ireland.

Marble is pure white so long as no other material is present. The most famous example of this is Carrera marble from Italy, as used by Michelangelo. More commonly there are impurities present, and these give us the large variety of coloured marbles from Europe that we see in the cathedrals and churches of Britain today.

Marble is a metamorphic rock, from a Greek word meaning literally a change of form. This total change of the original com-position of the limestone leaves a fine-grained, compact and very even

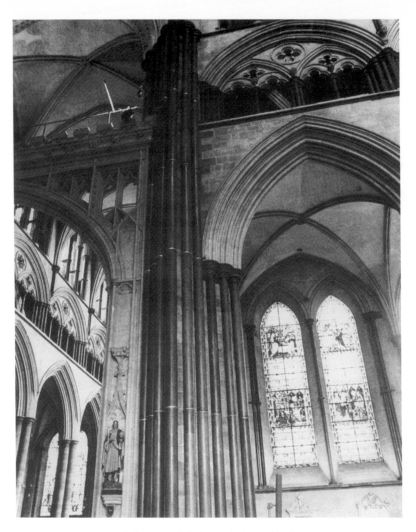

Salisbury Cathedral: Purbeck marble shafts

structure for the marble. This, combined with its ability to take a high polish, has made marble a much sought-after material.

The Greeks built most of their major temples with marble

because of the 'exactness of line'. They knew about the phenomenon of optical illusion and had even solved it by careful geometric adjustments. (One example is the *entasis* of tall columns, whereby they are deliberately made fatter in the middle compared with the top and bottom. If the columns were straight up and down, to our eyes they would appear concave.)

Purbeck marble is a material you will often hear mentioned in connection with buildings all over England. It comes from the Isle of Purbeck in Dorset, a few miles along the coast from Portland, but it is not a true marble. It is in fact a very fine and pure oolitic limestone, which has a resemblance to marble. In its unpolished state it is grey in appearance, and when polished and varnished it can almost appear black. Although not a true marble, it was widely used as such, especially in the 13th century when almost every major church in England contained it. Later, in Victorian times, it once again became fashionable and much sought after.

ALABASTER

ANOTHER STONE, resembling marble, has also been widely used in churches. This is alabaster, and if you've ever broken an arm, leg or collar-bone then you've been carrying a load of alabaster around without realising it. For alabaster is gypsum, the principal ingredient of plaster of Paris.

The North Midlands and the Trent valley are the major quarry sites for this soft, translucent stone. There are two main colours: a creamy white, and a honey colour which is less popular. The major use of alabaster was for tombs and effigies in the Middle Ages, just after the Black Death, and it also made a revival during the Victorian period when it was sometimes used for fonts, pulpits and other fixtures.

CHAPTER FIVE

Monasteries and Abbeys

WE HAVE SEEN that regular cathedrals were part of the whole monastic system, so let us look in more detail at the fascinating history of the monasteries themselves. They were a familiar and influential feature of everyday life in Britain for over a thousand years, until their dissolution by Henry VIII in 1540.

THE FIRST CHRISTIAN MONASTERIES

THE VERY FIRST Christian monks were solitary hermits who lived out in the Egyptian desert to escape from the oppression of the Roman Empire. The word monk derives from the Greek *monos* meaning alone. Over time individual hermits came to live together – the first group is attributed to St Anthony in 280 – and their communal way of life was copied. From Egypt the monastic life spread through Italy, North Africa, to France, and also to the isolated Celtic communities in the north of Britain (St Columba at Iona, for example).

In 529 St Benedict founded the monastery at Monte Cassino in the mountains between Naples and Rome. He drew up a set of regulations for the monks under him, and these rules were almost universally adopted as the basis of all monastic life in later centuries, especially after they had received the support and approval of Pope Gregory. These regulations came to be known as the Benedictine Rule, and the monks who lived by them were known as Benedictine monks.

It was Pope Gregory who introduced Benedictines to England when he sent St Augustine and his missionaries here. They founded the first Benedictine monastery at Canterbury in the year 598, and in spite of the later Anglo-Saxon invasions, it was from here that all the other Benedictine monasteries owed their origin.

Previous page: *Jedburgh Abbey, Scotland*

Benedictines

THERE WERE 500 monasteries in England by 1150 and later more than a thousand were built. Most of the major ones were for Benedictines. These included Canterbury, Durham, Norwich, Winchester, Gloucester, St Albans, plus the abbeys of Westminster, Bath and Tewkesbury. The Benedictine layout of monasteries is therefore the most dominant in Britain. The monks were known as 'Black monks' from the colour of their habits.

The Benedictine Rule was established during an age of great religious fervour, but with the passing of hundreds of years its observance became relaxed. At different times there were various attempts to re-establish the original routines and practices. Each of these attempts at reform gave rise to a new order of monks, each following its own Rule broadly based on those of Benedict.

Cluniacs

THE MOTHER CHURCH of the Cluniacs was founded in 910 at Cluny in Burgundy, with the intention of restoring the original aims and rules of St Benedict. This order first appeared in England around the year 1070. At the dissolution of the monasteries four and a half centuries later there were 32 Cluniac priories; Barnstaple being the earliest and Lewes the greatest. Two of the finest ruins of their buildings are at Much Wenlock in Shropshire and Castle Acre Priory in Norfolk; the latter is a wonderful example of Romanesque or Norman building at its best and grandest. Like the Benedictines, the Cluniacs were known as 'Black monks'.

Cistercians

THIS ORDER WAS FOUNDED in 1098 at Citeaux, also in Burgundy, partly as a protest against the ritualism of the Cluniacs and the learn-

Fountains Abbey: east end, Chapel of the Nine Altars

ing of the Benedictines, but principally against the slackness and corruption that had again crept into these older orders. The Cistercian monks became known as 'White monks' on account of the colour of their robes. Their first house in England was Waverley Abbey in Surrey, built in 1129, followed soon by many others.

A secluded site was always chosen for the Cistercian monastery, following the teaching of St Bernard: 'Our fathers searched out the damp and low lying valleys wherein to build their monasteries, so that the monks, being often in ill health and having death before their eyes, should not lead a careless life'. And so it was to the bare empty valleys of Yorkshire, Wales and Dartmoor that the Cistercians headed, to found the great abbeys of Fountains, Rievaulx, Kirkstall, Valle Crucis, Tintern, Buckfast and many others.

The planning and layout of the monasteries of all three of these orders – Benedictine, Cluniac and Cistercian – was basically the same, so if we walk around any of them today it is extremely difficult to tell at a glance and without prior knowledge which we are in.

Carthusians

THERE IS NO MISTAKING the distinctive plan of the Carthusians, so-called from the name of their monastery, the Charterhouse. If it was austerity, silence, coarse-haired shirts and vegetarianism that you were after, then the Carthusians was the order for you. They were founded in 1086, but never attained more than ten monasteries in this country. The monks lived in small cells (unlike the communal dormitories of the three previous orders) situated around the cloister. Each monk lived alone in his cell, praying, studying and writing, and even cooking his own vegetables grown in his personal garden adjacent to his cell. Although there was a communal dining-hall, both this and the small church was hardly used.

Mount Grace Priory in Yorkshire and Witham Priory in Somerset (the original Charterhouse in England) are good examples of the distinctive Carthusian layout.

THE MONKS' WAY OF LIFE

ONE OF THE KEYS to understanding what we find in a monastery building is the daily routine of the monks and their observance of the Rules. Their day from sunrise to sunset was divided into 12 'hours', the length of the 'hour' varying with the seasons. Of paramount importance to the monks was their duty to recite the seven services of the Liturgy. This meant seven separate visits to the church where they stood, knelt, or perched on their 'mercy-seats', the misericords, in the stalls of the choir whilst the service was read or sung.

Starting at midnight the monks were woken by the dormitory bell summoning them to the service of Matins ('morning'). This was followed by the service of Lauds, so-called because the three psalms sung during this service all began with the Latin word *Laudate*, meaning praise. The brothers then returned to bed.

The second bell of the day woke them at about 6 o'clock, sunrise, to call them to the service of Prime (the 'first hour'), followed by the morning Mass. This completed, they proceeded to the chapter-house for the daily meeting, where the abbot dealt with the business of the day.

After chapter came work, either around the monastery, on the adjacent farm, or in copying manuscripts for the highly-regarded monastic library. The next service Terce (the 'third hour') was followed by High Mass, which in turn was followed by the service at the 'sixth hour', Sext.

It was now mid-day and at last the monks could break their fast and retire to the refectory for the main meal of the day. The rest of the afternoon was again spent in work until the bell rang for the Nones, the normally-short service at the 'ninth hour'. At the 'tenth hour' came Vespers (the 'evening star') or Evensong where, as the name suggests, the service was sung. This was followed by the second meal of the day, supper, then back to the cloister until sunset, the 'twelfth hour', when they once again entered the church for the last time that day for the final service of Compline to 'complete' the day. This service contained the haunting incantation to the Virgin Mary, the *Salve Regina*. Then it was time for bed. After a short sleep in summer or a much longer one in winter, the midnight bell roused them for Matins and the daily cycle started again.

Seven times a day the monks were summoned to the church, 365 days a year, year after year, century after century. The bell rang, habits were put on, and feet shuffled silently toward the choir stalls without a word being spoken. This then was the world of the monk. A life devoted totally to God and unconcerned with the world outside.

Worcester: carved bosses on the cloister ceiling

We saw the influence the monastic system of prayers and services had on the shape and form of the eastern end of a cathedral. Now we are going to see how the rest of the monastic life led to a variety of buildings being specifically designed and constructed, such as the cloisters, chapter-house, dormitory, refectory, and many others, each with their own special function, which resulted in their own distinctive shape, size and position in relation to the church.

THE CLOISTERS

THE CLOISTERS are perhaps the most evocative of all the monastic ruins left from the past. To us they seem meditative as we walk through them, but what was their original function and why was their shape normally rectangular?

Traditionally the cloisters were built to the south of the church, and hence the north side of the cloister was the south wall of the church. The earliest cloisters were made of wood, and consisted of

*Fountains: looking across the garth; on the left are the arches
that lead to the chapter-house, on the right is the arch that leads to the refectory,
the well is in the centre*

four passageways or alleys. They had many uses. First and foremost they were covered walkways connecting individual buildings of the monastery and they were a part of the route used for the processions on Sundays and feast days. They were also used as a workplace for the monks, principally for the copying of manuscripts.

The square of grass in the middle of the cloister called 'the garth' would have been used for growing fruit, vegetables and herbs, of which great use was made, both for cooking and medicinal purposes. There was often a well in the garth, either in the centre, as at Fountains Abbey, or in one corner.

The eastern passageway of the cloister has two doorways leading from it, and behind these doorways lie two of the most important buildings for the monks. On the ground floor is the chapter-house and directly above it is the dormitory or dorter.

Worcester: chapter-house, the central column with the arched lines of ribbed vaulting that span the whole ceiling

THE CHAPTER-HOUSE

THE CHAPTER-HOUSE

THE CHAPTER-HOUSE was where the monks met every day after morning Mass. They filed out of the church in procession, along the east cloister, and then walked through a richly decorated doorway, which emphasised the hall's importance. The name comes from the fact that each day the meeting started with the reading of a chapter of the monastic Rule: if appropriate this was followed with a reading commemorating the saint of that day. The meeting then commenced with the obituaries of any monks who had died (the necrology). It was now the turn of a monk who wished to confess any misdemeanour to do so in public. Their 'crimes' were discussed by all, and the appropriate 'punishment', usually a penance, decided upon. Afterwards came the general business of running the monastery, and any farms and lands it owned. Leases, arbitration in disputes between tenants, and any other matters that were of importance to the smooth running of the foundation would be discussed.

The shape and decoration found within a chapter-house can easily become a study all of its own, as each is so highly individual and distinctive. Often the best solution to housing all the monks for their meetings was to make the chapter-house either circular, octagonal or polygonal in shape, and good examples can still be seen at Wells, Salisbury and Worcester. In the middle of the room at Worcester we can see one central column: from its top radiates an explosion of ribbed vaulting that spans and holds up the whole ceiling before coming to rest on the wall that surrounds the chamber. This fountain-head design is first and foremost a practical one, but as we have so often seen, the master-masons at the same time as solving a particular problem created immense beauty. For this reason chapter-houses are one of my favourite places.

Opposite: *Wells chapter-house, the central pier radiates its vaulting shafts like a mighty oak tree*

THE DORMITORY OR DORTER

A BOVE THE CHAPTER-HOUSE on the upper floor was the monks' sleeping room, the dormitory or dorter, which we can reach from the cloister by a stairway. In early monasteries they were very simple, long chambers, resembling a barrack-room, with little or no privacy. Later they were designed to be partitioned into separate cubicles with the emphasis on private study, meditation and prayer.

Here the monks would rise at midnight as the bell called them to Matins. In the dark they would make their way to the eastern end of the church to take up their positions in the choir stalls. They would go by way of the 'night stairs' which led straight from the dorter down into the transept of the church – a vital link between rest and prayer.

Leading off the side of the dorter and on the same level was the 'rere-dorter' or monastic lavatory, with individual cubicles along both sides of a central passageway. Not surprisingly, underneath the rere-dorter was the great drain of the monastery.

THE REFECTORY OR FRATER AND LAVATORIUM

I F WE RETURN to the cloisters by way of the 'day stairs' and continue on our way round the next corner, we find ourselves in the south cloister passageway. This leads us to the two features of this side, the lavatorium and the refectory. It is interesting that both the Old French (*fraitur*) and Latin (*refectorium*) names have survived for what we now refer to as a dining-room.

Before going in to eat the monks would wash their hands and faces, and so we find the lavatorium in front of, and adjacent to, the doorway of the frater. Details within the lavatorium of individual monasteries varied immensely, but essentially there was a large lead

Opposite: *Gloucester – the rich fan-vaulted ceiling of the lavatorium*

THE LAVATORIUM

Fountains: the refectory, the raised arches on the right
are part of the ruined pulpit

water-pipe, often with brass taps, running into a shallow basin. If the monastery was rich, this could even be faced with marble. At Fountains Abbey in Yorkshire we can still get a good idea of a typical arrangement, whilst at Gloucester Cathedral we can see the grandest of all, which even has its own little fan-vaulted ceiling.

In the refectory we would have found the abbot and prior and other monastic officials sitting at one table, usually raised up on a small platform. Above them on the wall would be a large painted or carved crucifix. At right angles to this high table were other tables down the full length of the room where the monks sat in collegiate style. Their mid-day meal would have been extremely welcome, for remember that they had not eaten for around fifteen hours.

The meals were eaten in silence, save for one voice. This came from the monk who stood in a specially-built pulpit in the side wall, raised above the tables, and read from the Scriptures or Homilies.

Some of these pulpits were plain and simple affairs, others as at Fountains Abbey were highly decorated. Two of the best examples can be seen in Chester and at Beaulieu Abbey in Hampshire.

If we stand in the refectory at Fountains Abbey and look around us, we might be forgiven for describing it at first glance as an empty stone chamber. But let's look a little closer. By using the history we have just learned, and our imagination, it can be transformed.

Fountains was a Cistercian abbey. That means we are unlikely to find much decoration here compared with a Benedictine abbey. On the right-hand side we can see the stone stairs that lead up to the pulpit where the monk read from the Scriptures during meals. If we climb up there and put ourselves in his position we can now see a large tall open window on the south wall. This was purely functional. It was placed where it would yield the best and longest exposure of natural light. Pick a ceiling of your choice; here in the frater they were usually of wood. Then imagine eighty or so hungry monks sitting in their white robes, arranged at the tables as we have already seen. Now we have created a very different room indeed.

THE CELLARIUM

BACK IN THE CLOISTER, we continue around the next corner to the west range of buildings, of which the largest and most interesting is the cellarium, also known as an undercroft. This was a large stone vaulted chamber, usually stretching the whole length of the west side of the cloister, in which were kept the stores of food and drink. The food was principally a good variety of fresh fruit and vegetables, grown either in the monastery gardens, on nearby farms belonging to it, or from estates further afield. There were also preserved meats, and both salted and fresh fish from their own fish ponds. Casks of beer, ale and wine were of great importance as they were drunk at nearly every meal. There are good records that have been passed down to us from the monks, known as the sacrist's rolls or account books, which

Fountains: the cellarium in a vaulted undercroft

carefully recorded everything contained in the cellarium. And what the monastery couldn't produce it either bartered for or bought at local fairs, markets or the nearest trading post.

Above the cellarium was a range of buildings used by the abbot and his guests. (In later times the abbot more commonly had a separate house built for himself somewhere in the monastery precincts.)

Mixed in and around this gastronomic south-west corner of the cloister were the necessary accessory buildings; the kitchen, pantry, buttery, bakery and the bolting house used to sieve and store corn.

THOSE THEN WERE the main eating, sleeping and meeting places of the monks that led from the cloister passageways. But there is one more range that we haven't looked at yet, and that is the north one, which lay along the south side of the church. As it was south-facing it was the lightest and warmest, especially as the early cloisters were unglazed. This was the site of the scriptorium. Here there would be carrels (wooden desks), each used by an individual monk as he copied and illuminated manuscripts to be used in the monastic library. Since the sale of these manuscript books was a good source of income, the scriptorium sometimes spread around the other cloisters, especially in the larger monasteries.

As well as these purely monastic buildings, there were many other rooms such as the infirmary and accommodation for lay-brothers who had their own dorter and frater, as well as guests' lodgings.

All in all the whole monastic layout, whose focal point was of course the church, could add up to a small or large village or even a town, as at Glastonbury where it occupied six acres.

THE RUINED CHAPTER-HOUSE AT FOUNTAINS ABBEY

I NOW WANT TO RETURN to Fountains Abbey so we can look more closely at the chapter-house — which most people pass by because they think there is nothing of interest there. Unlike the ones mentioned earlier which are still splendidly intact and still used for meetings (Wells, Salisbury and Worcester), the chapter-house at Fountains is a ruin, but because of this it offers us some exciting possibilities of reconstruction.

As a stone-mason I rather like this stone carcass of a monastery, for it offers the opportunity to see how it was put together, stone by stone. When restoring a church or part of a cathedral, I often come to places like this in order to refresh my memory and re-confirm the building techniques used in the medieval monastic plan. Walls, arches

Fountains: the chapter-house

and vaults can all be seen here in skeleton form, showing us exactly how they were built.

The first and most vital details to pick out are the stone projections (or corbels) that we can see placed at intervals around all the walls. These are the start of the original ribbed vaulting that spanned this room from one side to the other. Next we can see rows of marks on the ground where the columns were placed, and luckily for us there is even a surviving fragment of two of them. So, by the presence of rows of columns, we can see that this was not a central spanned roof like the ones we looked at earlier, and that in a way makes it even more interesting.

We are going to stand on the base of a broken column and become part of it, with our head serving as a capital. Looking toward

the side wall there is the start of the vault or the 'springer'. These are perhaps the most simple springers you will ever see, they are so close to us it is easy to use them to recreate the vaulted roof. Imagine the ribs rising from the springer up to the top of the boss, or keystone, then coming down the other side and finishing directly on top of us as the column. You could even design your own capital. (I myself am going to use one of those delightfully-simple fluted ones you can see on the ruined Galilee porch at the west front of the church.) And once you have vaulted the whole room, you can then add the monks sitting around the inside of the walls, dealing with the day's monastic business.

As with the refectory, this is an example of how we can combine the history we have learned and an eye for the details of the ruins that remain, and so recreate the past instead of just seeing a mound of stones that most people don't give a second glance. In other words, having been handed the keys to the masonry secrets of the past, we can now use them to unlock and reveal the treasures that lie within.

TOGETHER WE HAVE LOOKED at some of the most magnificent and majestic cathedrals and abbeys. So when I now mention the parish church you could be forgiven for thinking this may be something of an anticlimax. In fact the opposite is true. Although it may not have a stone-vaulted nave or an enormous spire or tower to impress and overwhelm us, it does have an intimate language all of its own. A small parish church will always surprise us. It is the combination of this intimate language and the accessible feeling which it radiates that gives the parish church its character. More importantly, it is generally unmolested by 'experts' who have turned their attentions to something more grand.

Now you know the basic rules you will soon recognise how the master-masons moulded them for their own particular uses. That is the fun and fascination of a parish church. Every one is individual. Of the thousands of churches I have either worked on or visited, I have never failed in some large or small way to be surprised and excited by the new secrets that lay waiting to be discovered.

Although parish churches and cathedrals share the same basic plan, it is important to realise just how different they are historically.

We have seen how the cathedral was built for the bishop and run by either a dean and chapter or by monks under the monastic system, and how for the most part it excluded the congregation. The parish church, however, was built specifically for the local people and their worship.

The building of the church was paid for by the lord of the manor who then appointed a priest to serve it and he was known as either a rector (ruler) or a parson (chief person). He was given a home, a piece of land called the 'glebe', and an annual sum of money, usually taken from the local tithe. Even before churches were built Christians set aside a tenth of their goods for the service of God. The priest now

Previous page: *Northlew, Devon — a rare complete rood screen with crucifix and door*

used these tenths or tithes to keep the church in repair, help the poor and show hospitality to visitors. Sometimes the lord of the manor gave the parish to a monastery which appointed its own priest to represent it, known as a vicar (vice or deputy), then the monastery took the greater part of the tithes, such as corn and wool, and the vicar had what was left over.

This was the basis on which parish churches evolved and it is little wonder that local people feel such a strong affinity for them even today. For centuries bells have rung from the church tower to speak to the local community; not just to call them to Mass but to mark the divisions of the day, for warnings, curfews and thanksgivings, and for baptisms, marriages and funerals.

A local parish church, however small or insignificant you may have thought it looked in the past, should now fill you with anticipation. As you walk towards the church you will know to which camp of learning you belong: either 'amateur academic' (pursues and remembers dates and terms with consummate ease), or 'hopeful enthusiast' (absorbs and remembers only one thing per visit but gets immeasurable pleasure from that one detail). Both are welcome and encouraged here. Many people ask me, 'Where do I start?' and to that question I always reply, 'Wherever you like!' There should be as few rules as possible when coming upon and taking in the often surprising delights of a church. We shall look at some of these together and see how and where they have fitted into the focal point of the town or village for the past thousand years, remembering of course that all churches are different and nearly all of them have been changed in subsequent centuries since our medieval starting point.

Crewkerne Church, Somerset

THE EXTERIOR

The Parapet

YOU CAN THINK OF the parapet as the decorative icing around the top edge of a cake, for it is the low wall that sits at the edge of all the roofs and runs around the whole of the church, even over the porch and tower roofs.

At first glance the parapet may not seem all that interesting, and even less so when you hear that its main function is to stop rainwater from flowing over the edge of the roof and running down the walls. But that is to underestimate its original importance which is revealed to us in the design of the top of the parapet. This repeated shape of a solid part and then an opening was used in military fortifications which is why it is called 'battlements'. The solid parts are called 'merlons', and the openings are called the 'embrasures'. The width of the embrasures would originally have been much smaller to allow the defending archer as much protection as possible while shooting his arrows. Later the battlements became purely decorative, and we find them with much wider spacings between the merlons, or uprights.

If the parapet has no battlements then it may have carved in it some of the many recurring decorative shapes we have become familiar with, such as the trefoil, quatrefoil or shapes from nature such as leaves and flowers. Whatever our parapet wall contains, positioned as it is on the edge of the roof and viewed from the ground, it is often silhouetted against the sky and this enhances its effect.

Gargoyles

ATTACHED TO THE BASE of the parapet and connected directly into the gutter behind it is the feature that more than any other illustrates the individuality, creativity and freedom of expression of the medieval stone-mason. The gargoyle's main function is to act as an extension of the rain gutter that runs behind the parapet, ensuring that this water is thrown several feet outwards from the walls below. The name derives from the French word *gorge* meaning throat and, although only occasionally visible, there is always a lead pipe running through the middle of the gargoyle and out through the throat and mouth of the carved figure.

Gargoyles are found all over the roofs around the church and tower, in an uncountable number of designs. There are hideous

THE PARISH CHURCH

Gargoyles: opposite *Cerne Abbas, Dorset;* clockwise from top left *Curry Rivel, Somerset; Loders, Dorset (two); and Sherborne Abbey*

grotesque faces, and unpleasant acts of torture or debauchery, or – in the best examples – a combination of all three. Binoculars are a must for the enjoyment of some of the gargoyles which are high up on the walls.

The Tower

TOWERS ARE wonderful structures, whatever their shape and size. They look down on the rest of the church fabric with a kind of authoritative nobility all their own. Whether they rise from the centre

Staple Fitzpaine, Somerset:
15th century tower

of the church, from the crossing, or stand majestically at the west end, they command respect. Towers had an ancient origin in military defence and were originally built as lookouts, but in later centuries their main function was as a belfry to hold the church bells.

The shape, size, and indeed the materials used in the construction of towers, all varied from region to region; in fact in some cases they have now become synonymous with a particular area. The round flint towers of East Anglia are a perfect example of this. There are limits to using flint as a building material, particularly in making the corners and buttresses of square towers, and this is reflected in the simple round shape of these towers that are both long-lasting and instantly identified with the skill of the flint-knappers in East Anglia.

But for the most beautiful and graceful examples of the towers of a particular region we have to go to Somerset and its surrounding area. Here we can find true craftsmanship combined with design which gives us not only the finest, but for me the most harmonious towers in the whole country.

Let us now have a proper look at a typical tower. Starting at the very top we notice that the tower is crowned with a parapet wall, and also has pinnacles at each corner. Later Gothic towers contained a huge embattled parapet together with numerous pinnacles to create towers with a crown of dramatic proportions that could be seen for miles around. At the bottom of the parapet will be the carved stone gargoyles.

A tower usually has three chambers on different floor levels within. We can tell where they are from the outside by using the 'string courses' as a guideline. The main job of a string course is to help shed water from the four faces of the tower. That is why it projects outwards and has a deeply-cut moulding underneath to act as a drip-stone. But it also tells us where the floors are in the tower.

The top division or 'chamber' of the tower is easily identified by the window which has louvred boards (sloping strips of timber) to allow out the sound of the bells which are hung inside. The higher the bells are hung, the further they can be heard. Either of the lower chambers could be used as the 'ringing chamber', where the bell-ringers stand and pull on the bell ropes.

At each corner of the tower there are buttresses, rising either to part or full height. Some buttresses are thick and heavy, some are light and slender. As they climb the tower most buttresses are stepped, which is the classic design of a support system, the strongest and widest part at the base, and the lightest at the top.

The way up the tower is by steps. This is an internal winding staircase of either stone or wooden steps. The stairs are hidden from our view and run up inside the 'stair turret' which can be seen from the outside. Sometimes this is just a simple round projection running the height of the tower at one of the corners. In later centuries it became highly-developed and takes the shape of a polygon (many sided) turret with its own parapet and pinnacles at the top, even higher and grander than the tower's own crown. In this elaborate state stair turrets stand out as a feature in their own right, and they gave the masons another opportunity to exercise their design and decorative skills.

Kilpeck, Herefordshire: a round-arched Norman doorway

Doorways

As we know, the shape and decoration of a doorway can give us a rough guide to the date it was built. This applies to a parish church as much as a cathedral. So we can look for the rounded Norman doorway and the three stages of pointed Gothic.

There is one different doorway that merits a special look, the priest's door. Found on the south side of the chancel wall it is often now filled in, but still clearly visible as a doorway. This was the priest's personal entrance because the clergy owned the chancel end of the church and the congregation owned the nave.

Right: *Othery, Somerset: priest's doorway*

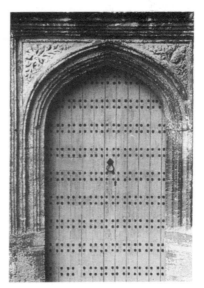

Left: *Crewkerne, Somerset: ogee-shaped arched doorway*
Right: *Staple Fitzpaine, Somerset, four-centred or Tudor arch*

THE EXTERIOR

Somerton, Somerset: the ground level windows are Decorated while the clerestory above is Perpendicular

Windows

As with doorways, windows also follow the three stages of Gothic plan. It is not uncommon to find all three types in one church, plus an original surviving Norman round-arched one, due to subsequent alterations to the fabric of the church. You have to keep your eyes peeled. If you are searching for that surviving little round-arched window, and believe me it is well worth the effort, then my advice is that it will probably be close to ground level, as later additions often occur to the higher parts and the roof. A small simple Norman window has much to offer us in the way of contemplation. When I see one I think of the master-mason trying to explain to the stone-masons in Norman-French how to build it when they only understood Anglo-Saxon.

Loders, Dorset: a 'head portrait' end stop to the hood-mould

Protection from Rain

THE DOORWAYS AND WINDOWS had their own form of protection from the weather in the use of a 'dripstone' or 'hood-mould'.

Just as our eyes are protected from rain by our eyebrows, so are the doorways and windows around the church protected by hood-moulds above them. They project outwards for anything from six inches to one foot to give that vital protection. The shape usually follows that of the window or doorway, with two major exceptions.

The first is the ogee shape of the Decorated period, and the second is in the Perpendicular period when the hood-moulds formed a rectangular covering to the window and doors below.

Where the hood-mould finishes on either side of the opening it covers, there are sometimes delightful carvings to be seen. Instead of simply finishing the moulding abruptly, the stone-masons realised that they could turn this 'end stop' into a feature; such as bunches of foliage, or masks, or even head portraits of the masons themselves. Carvings of kings, queens and bishops were also popular decorations.

Corbels

THE CORBEL is also a projecting stone that often contains carved figures and representations of nature. Its main job though is a structural one. A corbel (from the Latin *corbis* meaning a basket) was used

Gloucester Cathedral: corbels

to support a weight above it. Some of the most decorative corbels can be seen in the nave where they hold up and support the beginning of the vaulting shafts that make up the high vault.

Outside, corbels are best seen in a long row underneath the parapet wall or a cornice. This is known as a 'corbel table'.

Low-sided Windows

No OTHER LONG-FORGOTTEN feature of our medieval church history provides so much fruitful ground for conjecture as the curious and often mysterious 'low-sided window'.

Sometimes these are found high up on the wall of the chancel or nave but they are more often nearer ground level. Their position can be almost anywhere in the church; north, south or west, but not the east end. When they are found they usually provide contradictions to the various theories as to their original function. It is therefore

Othery, Somerset: this low-sided window has access through a buttress

difficult to give a common plan to which they all adhere, but as a general rule we can say that they are lower in height than the normal windows. They are usually found on the south side of the church either in the nave or at the beginning of the chancel where one would normally expect to find the priest's door. They usually have hinges that would have — or still do — hold wooden shutters. If there are no hinges or shutters then there is usually an iron grating across the aperture. These windows always open inwards, an important point to remember when we begin our detective work.

With so many variations to the plan and siting of these low-sided windows, it is no surprise to find that there is endless debate as to their function. Some theories that have been argued over include:

1. At Easter these low-sided windows enabled the lit Paschal Candle to be seen from outside.

2. They acted as a hagioscope so that the Elevation of the Host at the altar could be observed from outside.

3. The 'vulne' theory suggests they are an architectural feature symbolic of the Crucifixion wound of Christ (where the structure of the whole church represented Christ's body, as described earlier).

4. They were 'leper windows' allowing lepers to watch the Mass from outside the church, their presence inside not being welcome for obvious reasons.

5. They were 'confessional windows', with the priest inside the church and the penitent outside. And so the theories go on and on, everything from being used for the passing of alms to beggars to functioning as a ventilator permitting the escape of unpleasant fumes from newly-lit incense.

Here is my own explanation for these low-sided windows. In the Mass of the Roman Catholic Church the most holy and symbolic part is the Elevation of the Host. This is the point when the priest lifts the Sacrament high above the altar and the words 'Sanctus, sanctus, sanctus' are recited, the occasion being marked by the ringing of the Sanctus bell. The fact that these windows are usually found on the south side of the church, closest to the neighbouring village (or on the north side if the village was on that side) suggests to me that when the Elevation of the Host was reached, an attendant on the inside of the church would open the shutters of the window and ring the Sanctus bell through it. Everyone in the vicinity would therefore know that the critical point of the Mass had been reached and could join in by kneeling wherever they were at the time. The usual position of the low-sided window in the wall closest to the village would therefore be of importance in carrying the sound of the bell to where most inhabitants would be, especially those who were too ill or infirm to attend. In those occasional churches where this window is placed high up, then the bell would be fixed on the inside and pulled by a rope, the sound carrying in exactly the same way to the village.

Porches

A PORCH, be it large, small, grand, or quietly humble, is almost certain to be found at one or more of the entrances to a church.

The earliest church porches were found along the 'Pilgrims' Routes' in Burgundy and France, at such places as Tournes, St Benoit-sur-Loire and Cluny. They were usually situated at the west end of the nave and here they provided shelter to the pilgrims as they gathered, waiting to be shown around the church.

The porches were commonly known by two other names, the 'Narthex' and 'Galilee'. 'Narthex' was the term originally used for the enclosed space at the entrance to the catacombs in Rome dating from pre-Christian times, and as such is very ancient in use and meaning. It is seldom used today as people frown on its use as a religious term because of its pagan origin. The use of the name 'Galilee' for the porch derives from a Sunday ceremony of early times held in a cathedral. This was the weekly Festival of the Resurrection when the

Curry Rivel, Somerset: a porch with an upper storey and a stoup

bishop would lead his attendants 'in procession' into the church. This symbolised Christ leading his disciples into Galilee.

But what about our parish church porches? Here we find our strongest link with the ordinary people of the past. The church porch was a centre of village life in medieval times. It was a public meeting place particularly where parish affairs were concerned – remnants of this can still be seen by the display in the porch of 'public' notices, such as details of General, Local and Parish Elections.

What may surprise many people today is that various ceremonies were originally conducted in the porch before participants proceeded into the church for a Blessing. When a child was taken to be baptised, for example, the baby was received by the priest in the porch where the first part of the service was performed: only then did they go into the church for the remainder of the rite. Similarly, the first part of the service for the Churching of Women (purification after childbirth) was carried out in the porch. But perhaps the most surprising ceremony of all was that of marriage, where the principal 'binding' or 'troth-giving' part of the service was performed in the porch – in early Christian days this was usually carried out by a senior member of the bride and/or groom's family and not by the priest – before the newly-married couple went into the church for a Blessing on the marriage given by the priest. In *The Canterbury Tales* Chaucer wrote of his 'Wife of Bath':

> She was a worthy woman all her life,
> Husbands at church door had she five.

Many porches throughout the country, even of quite small churches, have an upper storey with a room which has served a variety of uses over the centuries. These were frequently the home – complete with fireplace – of a sacristan whose duties among others included the ringing of bells for services. The room frequently served as a strong room for the whole parish (there were no bank safe deposits in those days) where any valuables could be stored and also wills kept in safety. Other functions of this room — which was also known as a *parvise* or 'enclosed space' — was as an armoury, a library, a general lumber room and, after the Reformation, a church school. Some were later converted into small chapels.

Porches come in all shapes and sizes. Some are functional and some are plain, but nearly all have their own special atmosphere. Never think of them merely as a covering for the door of the church. They almost invariably have some beauty of their own. Some have their own tiny vaulted ceilings, others have stone carvings of a quite original flavour not seen elsewhere in the building. The masons, aware that people would often stop to talk here or merely pause for thought, realised that the porch was a place where they could express something of their own personality for people to look upon for a while.

Scratch or Mass Dials

THIS IS ONE DETAIL which can sometimes be found on the outside of churches that never fails to excite me. Very few dials are described in guidebooks for the simple reason that they are barely visible and very insignificant, even if they have survived. I have come across churches where their presence was unknown to the vicar or church-wardens. Little skill was needed to carve them — probably most were not carved by a professional stone-mason — but their simplicity and link with the past, combined with their rarity today, make for a truly magical find. Find is the operative word, for you first have to learn where to look for a dial. Simply go to the south side of the church, find the chancel end, and look for the priest's door (it may have been converted into a window, or if it is walled-up look for its position in the stonework). Now look closely to the right-hand side of this door-way at about head height. This is the most common place to find a dial, but it might be on a neighbouring buttress as a flat ashlar (squared stone) surface is needed.

So what are we looking for? We are trying to find a series of lines scratched into the surface radiating from a central point. They look something like sun-dials but are very different from them, although the sun's shadow is essential for both to function. Sun-dials only came into fashion at the end of the 17th or beginning of the 18th centuries, while these scratch or Mass dials are very much older. The name 'scratch dial' derives from the fact that the lines were 'scratched' into the stone rather than being carved, while the name 'Mass dial' indicates their original function of telling the congregation the time of the Mass on a particular day.

Bradford Abbas, Dorset: Mass dial

Mass dials appear in many forms, sizes and details as well as position, but in general they have a central hole from which the lines radiate. The lines are not at regular intervals as on a sun-dial, and there are far fewer of them. One line is usually deeper than the others, and this indicates the most common time for Mass, 9 a.m.: lesser lines indicate other times for Mass, and very rarely the hours are also marked. The priest would place a small stick known as a 'gnomon' into the hole in the middle of the scratch dial to indicate that there was to be a Mass that day and at a time when the sun's shadow reached the next 'Mass mark'. At the end of the service he would remove the gnomon.

The scratch dials we see today have usually been re-carved or rather re-scratched over many centuries. Sometimes there are a cluster of them together and occasionally they are found in and around other parts of the church, indicating that the original chancel has been rebuilt and the stone containing the scratch dial has been re-used

THE EXTERIOR

elsewhere. I have even come across ones that have been inserted upside-down, their original purpose long forgotten and fallen into disuse.

Most churches have been added to over the years, to a greater or lesser degree, but this particular part, the south wall of the chancel both outside and inside (we'll see later the treasures to be found on the inside) offers us the best chance to find a direct link to the past. When I stand at the priest's entrance to his chancel, looking at his scratch dial, it is not hard to sense a medieval rhythm and time that has long since evaporated. To stand and muse has always been one of my pastimes: it doesn't cost anything and indeed the longer one lingers and dreams, the richer one becomes.

I have taken great pleasure in re-scratching some of these ancient scratch dials, so that they can be preserved for the future.

Anchorite Cells

A RARE BUT INTERESTING feature occasionally found attached outside the cold north wall of a church is an anchorite's cell – or one for an anchoress. (An anchorite was male, an anchoress female.) These were people who were determined to devote themselves to a life of prayer away from their normal home, but did not wish to enter a monastery or nunnery. They did this in a cell attached to the outside wall of the church, usually little more than an added-on lean-to. They entered this stone cell and the doorway was walled-up after them. They remained in this *Domus inclusi* (enclosed home) for the rest of their lives, their only contact with the outside world being through a small window through which passed their food etc. Another small window linking them with the interior of the church enabled them to join in the services.

Anchorites should not be confused with hermits who were not restricted in a cell. These cells first appeared in Britain about the year 650. In 14th century records at Exeter Cathedral is included a special

Crewkerne, Somerset: this is thought to be an anchorite cell, it is set into the south-east corner of the church facing the town

service for the walling-up when an anchorite entered his or her cell. During this service, *Reclusio Ancoritarum*, the Extreme Unction was administered as in the ceremony for Burial of the Dead.

Surprisingly, there was no shortage of applicants to become an anchorite/anchoress. Monks, nuns, friars, parish priests, and even titled gentry took to the *Reclusiorum*. It was not always as simple a life as it might appear. For example, an aged anchoress at St Julian's, Norwich, by the name of Lady Julia had her two maids interred with her.

One useful service to the local community performed by these anchorites – or more usually by anchoresses – was of running a school for both boys and girls of the area. They taught the children to read and write by speaking to them through the external window, and the small pittance they received for doing this paid for their food and other needs.

INSIDE THE CHURCH

WHEN WE ENTER the parish church it is worth remembering how closely it relates to the plan and layout of a great cathedral. There are, however, two major differences to bear in mind.

Tarrant Rushton, Dorset: a squint on each side of the chancel arch

Bradford Abbas, Dorset: chancel screen

First you probably won't find a stone vaulted roof in the nave or the side aisles, and so there won't be any triforium or flying buttresses to see either, since they are the supporting parts to a stone vaulted roof. Instead we are likely to see a wooden ceiling overhead. Second, the east end of the church, the altar end, which is known in the cathedral as the choir, sanctuary or presbytery, is simply referred to in the parish church as the chancel from the Latin word *cancellus* meaning screen. Generally the whole eastern end of the parish church is referred to as the chancel, including the arch above its entrance which is known as the chancel arch.

The journey which we took together through the cathedral from the beginning of the nave to the east end can equally be followed here in the parish church. You'll find the same columns, capitals and decorative elements, such as quatrefoils, trefoils, and nature's influence on the carving in the form of flowers or foliage, used all over the fabric of the church to bring to life the stone, wood and wrought-iron.

The details we shall be looking at together are some you may not have been aware of before, or indeed heard of, such as the sedilia, the piscina and a squint. I have deliberately chosen these small but intimate objects because they are often passed over by many guides or not explained properly, and because they offer us an insight into medieval life.

Please take one other thought with you as you enter the parish church. Remember that the smaller and simpler the church, the more intimate and tactile it becomes. It may have no aisles or transepts, but that should not diminish our enthusiasm. On the contrary, it means it is less complicated and therefore clearer for us to read. Each church however small will have something of interest lying in wait for you to discover.

The Squint or Hagioscope

WE ARE NOW going to look at, or rather look through, another feature that while redundant in modern times was a part of the medieval Mass. We know that a rood screen was the partition that separated the nave (congregation) from the east end (clergy). The most important part of the Mass was the Elevation of the Host, but the screen prevented it from being seen by the congregation. A solution was found by introducing a squint. To the side of the rood screen – usually the south side, but occasionally the north or even both sides – an opening was cut, about three feet wide on the nave side tapering through the thickness of the wall to less than one foot wide on the chancel side. This narrow-view passage enabled a person standing on the nave side to have a view of the altar – but not much else – and so observe the precise moment of the raising of the Host. He was then able to indicate this sacred act to the rest of the congregation by ringing the Sanctus bell.

Powerstock, Dorset: a squint looking towards the altar

Many of these squints have now been filled in and plastered over, but their outlines can sometimes be determined. If they still exist it is worthwhile looking through them to see which part of the chancel is visible. Remember that originally they were built to give a view of the altar. If this is not now visible, then it may well indicate that the chancel has been altered.

The name 'squint' is the older one, the Greek word 'hagioscope' was only introduced in the last century.

Piscina

PISCINAS ARE FOUND on the south wall next to the altar. They are shallow stone basins either set into or projecting from the wall, and there is a hole at the bottom to release whatever water is poured in. They are small and at waist height and were used for washing the priest's hands.

The form and decoration of these piscinas also decide their date, Early English and Decorated being the most common. You may find more than one bowl in these little niches: two bowls are not uncommon, and three is a real find. There may also be a small wooden shelf behind the bowl, to place newly-washed vessels on, such as the chalice, before they were used in the service. This was called a 'Credence shelf'. Piscinas with two bowls were designed so that the priest could wash his hands in one bowl, and the vessels in the other.

The word *piscina* is a good example of how a present-day word has derived from the classical language. I remember my first evening at an Italian class. The teacher constructed a sentence saying that we were all going to take a trip to the 'piscina'. 'Now does anyone know what that means?' she asked hopefully. With my stone-mason's knowledge, I replied that it was 'a basin in the wall of a church, Signorina'. She peered over the top of her spectacles, and paused for a moment as if to make sure that I was one of her students, and not someone who had wandered in by accident from the Building Department. With a furrowed brow she simply replied 'No!', and it was only when she revealed that we were going to the swimming baths that the connection hit me. In modern Italian *piscina* is 'a swimming pool'. In the Latin of Ancient Rome, *piscina* was 'a fish pond, a pond, or a trough'. The *piscina* of our churches came from the Christians of Ancient Rome, where a lead trough served the purpose.

Compton Martin, Somerset:
Norman piscina

Stoup

ANOTHER STONE BASIN is the stoup, used to contain holy water in churches before the Reformation. These are found, often set into a corner, either inside or outside the porch entrance and the congregation upon entering and leaving the church would dip their hands into the water and cross themselves. A stoup can look similar to a piscina though they are usually much plainer and without the drain hole in the bottom.

Kilpeck, Herefordshire: this stoup may
be pagan in origin

Font

JUST INSIDE THE CHURCH doorway or at the west end of the church will be the font, which can be one of the oldest fixtures of the church. There is a good survival rate for Norman and even a few Saxon fonts that are interesting both in shape and history. These were made deep and broad and much lower than later ones. This was because people actually stood or knelt inside them to be baptised with holy water, and a child would be fully immersed. The familiar simple strong solid details of the Norman style were carved on the outside of these deep broad fonts making them easy to recognise – and they are an exciting find as you can imagine someone kneeling inside being showered with water. Early fonts were usually lined with lead, and there are thirty or so in the country that are made solely of lead and sit on a stone pedestal. All of them had a stopper and plughole that allowed the water to escape.

Milborne St Andrew, Dorset: Norman font,
(right) Altarnun, Cornwall: granite Norman font

*Pershore Abbey, Worcestershire (top) Winterborne Steepleton, Dorset (left)
and Toller Fratrum, Dorset; Norman fonts*

In 1236 Edmund, Archbishop of Canterbury decreed that all fonts should be covered or locked and the key held by the parish priest. Before this time there were no covers and it was said that holy water was being stolen by witches who used it in their pagan rituals.

Later Gothic fonts are taller and shallower with fine intricate carving on the outside. The covers also became very tall and highly decorated and are made mainly of wood.

Sedilia

THE NAME SEDILIA is derived from the Latin word for 'seat', and these stone seats are invariably found on the south side of the chancel close to the piscina. Victorian 'restorers' usually added some steps up to the altar, and frequently this has partially hidden a beautifully-carved sedilia. Although the number of seats can vary there are

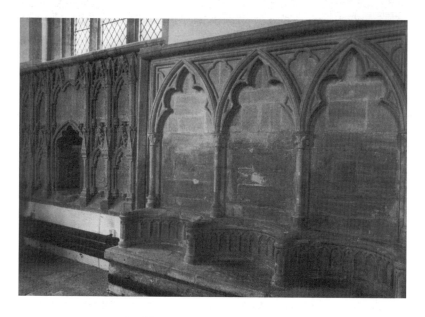

Isle Abbots, Somerset: sedilia and piscina

Exeter Cathedral: stepped triple sedilia with piscina in the left corner

most commonly three, one each for the priest and his two assistants, the deacon and sub-deacon. The seats were usually at different heights according to rank, and the clergy sat there during certain parts of the Mass.

The seats were usually of carved stone and recessed into the south wall to form a kind of niche. The most ancient type was a single stone slab projecting from the wall. Since it was so simple, it was too plain for later 'restorers' and their consequential removal is the reason that so few early sedilia remain. The decoration of later sedilia takes many forms: quatrefoils, trefoils, or some form of simple tracery are the usual designs that were constructed over the tops of the seats, while thin long shafts or narrow columns separate one seat from the other.

The Easter Sepulchre

THE EASTER SEPULCHRE was a representation of Christ being laid in the tomb after his death on the Cross. It took the form of a recess in the north wall of the chancel in which a crucifix was placed throughout the holy days of Easter. These recesses can easily be found today because, as you can imagine, it was an opportunity for the craftsmen to make a simple opening in the wall into something of splendour and decoration worthy of representing and signifying the rebirth of Easter. On Good Friday a crucifix was placed in the sepulchre and two candles were lit in front of it. Parish records show that men were paid to stay inside the church and watch over the sepulchre until the Vigil was completed before dawn on Easter Sunday with a Service of Light. Instead of a decorated recess in the wall, some churches had a permanent elaborately carved stone tomb which would be used in the same way.

Opposite: *Loders, Dorset – a simple Easter sepulchre set into the north wall of the chancel,* above, *Crediton, Devon: a highly-decorated Easter sepulchre*

Sanctuary and the Frithstool

IN MEDIEVAL TIMES the church building always offered sanctuary to people accused of a crime until the time that they stood trial. This prevented anyone from being summarily killed by a 'lynch mob', and also enabled the person to gather his defence together. The main door was the first part of the church reached by the fugitive, and at this point he could claim the privilege of sanctuary and be safe from any

Durham Cathedral: sanctuary knocker, 12th century

pursuing hue and cry. The door handle is still occasionally referred to as a 'sanctuary knocker'. Very rarely in a church we come across the second stage of this sanctuary, the frithstool, 'the stone seat of peace' placed close to the altar. There is a superb example at Beverley Minster, possibly of Norman origin, with an inscription carved on it offering peace and security to any fugitive reaching it. *Haec sedes lapidea Freedstoll dicitur i.e. pacis cathedra, ad quam reus fugiendo perveniens omnimodam habet securitatem.* (This stone seat is known as the Frithstool i.e. the chair of peace, when a fugitive reaches it he is granted absolute security.)

Pulpit

THE MEDIEVAL PULPIT was mostly to be found on top of the rood screen from where the priest could address the people in the nave. These early pulpits have nearly all disappeared and the ones we can see today date from after the Reformation when the sermon became of more importance. An edict of 1603 stated that every church should be provided with 'a comely and decent pulpit'. Most pulpits were built at around this time and are made of wood or stone, or even marble or alabaster in a rich parish or a cathedral. They were a fine place for the stone or woodcarvers to practise their skill.

My own favourite part of the pulpit is the capping or wooden hat that is suspended above the speaker's head. Its purpose is as a sounding board to throw the preacher's voice out to the congregation.

Benchends

THERE WERE NO PEWS or seating in the parish church until well into the 16th century, the only exception being a few benches set against the wall for the infirm. This incidentally is the origin of the saying 'The weakest go to the wall'.

Altarnun, Cornwall: late-medieval oak benchends

Trent, Dorset: early 16th century benchends

When pews and benches were introduced they were often decorated by the local woodcarver. The West Country seems to be particularly rich in imaginative carvings. As the first seated benches changed from simple plain planks of oak into the highly ornate and finished pews we see today sometimes a detail called a 'poppyhead', from its similarity to the poop of a ship, was added on the top of the end pew. This rose upwards in a very ornate way and gave a distinct finial appearance to the benchend.

THE CHURCHYARD

You will often hear the churchyard referred to as God's Little Acre. This is in fact the original size of the piece of land set aside for it. Medieval churchyards contained no headstones but since the church was the focal point of the village community the land was used for fairs, markets and even archery practice. If the churchyard is oval or circular in shape this is likely to mean that it pre-dates the church building and was originally a site of pagan worship which was taken over by the early Christians and incorporated into the Church. These are not uncommon and it is worth looking out for them. Yew trees are features of old churchyards. The explanations given for this are many. My own opinion is that because they are evergreen and long lived (it is claimed there are yews as old as 2000 years) they were also used in pagan rites and later adopted by the Church.

Beaminster, Dorset: tower and churchyard

We saw earlier how all the interesting details were found on the south side of the church and so it is with the land that lies around it. On the south side are most of the headstones that started to become common around 1600, while on the north side there are usually few and here were often buried the unbaptised or even suicides or murderers. This was because the north side was in shadow most of the day and people shied away from this part of the yard. When you look at headstones – another example of the stone-mason's art – notice that they are almost all facing east so that as the sun rotates it casts a better shadow on the incised letters and makes them easier to read.

Epilogue

IN THE MODERN WORLD of today we find ourselves bombarded and overpowered by the visual images of a mass media intent on delivering its messages in a way that at best can be described as overwhelming, and at worst as disturbing. So it is little wonder that we look back to the long-forgotten medieval past for a relief from the pace of life today.

The romantic image of the original builders of the cathedrals has been brought about by a progression of myths arising from the need for people to identify with smiling, contented and almost heroic craftsmen. We should therefore recognise that medieval life of any kind was harsh, insecure and often perilous. Time, and the life and death struggle it brought, was counted very much from day to day, and not from year to year, whether you plied your trade as a stone-mason, wool merchant or goldsmith, or were the lowest type of peasant. Bearing in mind this day-to-day struggle to keep body and soul alive, the achievement in building the magnificent medieval stone structures we see today appears even more incredible, and words like 'dynamic', 'awesome' and 'sensational' sit easily in their true perspective.

But now it is not just the fabric of the building that excites and enthrals us, it is also the medieval rhythm of life that we can sense as we begin to understand more about how to read a building. Remember the scratch or Mass dial and its use as a time piece, or the church porch and the differing roles it played in a way of life now almost totally gone.

To end our journey together I have chosen one of my favourite buildings. This is the little parish church of St Andrew at Winterborne Tomson, set in the isolated rural landscape of Dorset.

At first sight there doesn't seem much to set the pulses racing, but let's look a little closer. There is not a single ounce of decoration to be seen anywhere on the outside: no parapets, no gargoyles, and no intricate carving to be immediately admired. Only three plain windows pierce the south wall. So let's use some of the rule of thumb guides we have learned to discover why this austere-looking little church is so exciting.

The east end (closest to us as we approach) is a semi-circular apse. This immediately tells us that the building is Norman in origin, and that we are dealing with something constructed around the year 1100. For me, that beautiful semi-circular curve that shapes both the wall and the roof provides the most simple and graceful ending to be found on any building. If we add to its smooth sweeping curve the fact that this basilica shape had its origins deeply and directly rooted in Ancient Rome, then this unassuming little church sitting quietly and peacefully as it does in the English landscape starts to take on a whole different significance. Here before us in the 20th century is a building dating from nearly a thousand years ago, which in turn was based on what existed a thousand years before, in the earliest days of Christianity.

When we first looked at cathedrals we saw that the Norman work was also called 'Romanesque' and that we could find the shapes and forms of a mighty cathedral in the most humble of village churches. Winterborne Tomson is a very good example of both.

Let's look at those three windows that have been inserted at a much later date than the rest of the fabric. The square-headed moulding above the windows tells us that at a rough guess they were added around 1550 or later. It could be argued that because they pierce the wall in such a drastic fashion they detract from the stark, simple, solid, early feel to the church. But we can also see how the progression of the centuries and the changes of shapes and styles leave their mark, just like an indelible fingerprint. Few medieval buildings have escaped the additions or rebuilding of later years, and that is of course one of the things that make them so fascinating.

The inside has also been touched by the hand of later additions. The oak ribs of the roof are cleverly and delicately cut to radiate and emphasise the curve of the apse. The box pews, screen and pulpit are all early 18th century and are also of oak, their light appearance is due to lime, sunlight and the wear of nearly three centuries. These clean simple lines and almost austere appearance sit quite happily in this interior of beautiful intimate serenity.

Although the walls of this little Dorset church are devoid of any decoration, they are in fact made up of a wonderful array and mixture of different types of stones found in the West Country. Gold- and silver-coloured limestones, green sandstones, chalk, flint, and a host of others that form a patchwork of contrasts and contradictions both in colour and in the way they have been laid one on top of another.

So there you have it, my friends. One of the smallest and humblest churches at first sight can soon become a microcosm of history spanning nearly two thousand years. This is just one example of the treasures that lie waiting to be unveiled throughout the length and breadth of the country. Whether it is a large and majestic cathedral or a humble collection of random stones left open to the elements, they are all waiting to be discovered and enjoyed by *you*.

As I sit on the churchyard wall gazing at these wonderful shapes while thinking about the medieval craftsmen and changing rhythms of history that brought them here, I can think of only one word to describe such contentment and serenity, and that is sheer and utter 'Benediction'.

Index

Numbers in **bold** refer to illustrations

INDEX

Acknowledgments

I AM VERY GRATEFUL to my editor, Jenny Cottom, for all the assistance, care and encouragement she has given me throughout; and to Peter Ward whose elegant design of the text and photographs has added so much to the book.

I also want to thank the following people who have all been involved in various ways: Alison Ayres, Helen Baz, Susan Bennett, Ken Eglin, Anna Enayat, Olwyn Foot, Margaret Grant and Diana Trenchard.

I am grateful to the Deans and Chapters of the Cathedrals at Durham, Exeter, Gloucester, Norwich, Salisbury, Wells, Winchester and Worcester for giving me permission to take photographs.

Lastly I want to thank Gudrun Nickel for her support and patience; without it I would never have achieved this.

T.M.
Bridport, Dorset
All Saints Day 1996